W9-CXN-798

SUPER BOWL!

SUPERSTARS AND SUPER STORIES

by Michael E. Goodman

Troll Associates

For Amanda, who helps make each day a little more super.

Super Sunday

At 1:30 in the morning on January 3, 1972, most people in Miami, Florida, were asleep—but not Don Shula. Shula was the coach of the Miami Dolphins football team. He was awake watching films of both his own club and the Dallas Cowboys, who would be squaring off in Super Bowl VI in New Orleans in less than two weeks.

Suddenly the phone rang in Shula's house. "I wonder who that could be at this hour," he thought. A voice at the other end of the line said, "Coach Shula, the president is calling." It seemed that President Richard Nixon was also up late that night and was also thinking about the upcoming Super Bowl game. He had a suggestion for a passing play the Dolphins might use against Dallas. "I think you can hit Paul Warfield on a down-and-in pattern and score," Nixon said.

A few days later, Dallas coach Tom Landry received a telegram from former president Lyndon Johnson, a fellow Texan. It read: "My prayers and my presence will be with you in New Orleans, although I don't plan to send you any plays."

The two presidents were among millions of Americans

1

whose attention throughout most of January was focused on one event, the Super Bowl—the championship game of professional football. The day on which the Super Bowl occurs is almost like a holiday in the United States. In fact, the day has been given its own special name: "Super Sunday." Shopping areas are usually deserted, highways are uncrowded, and police departments even report a reduction in crime on Super Sunday. Television ratings soar, and advertisers spend millions of dollars on commercials to get viewers of the game to buy their products.

The Super Bowl is America's youngest professional sports championship, but it's the one that gets the most attention from the media and from sports fans. Unlike the other championships, the Super Bowl is a one-day event. Win and you're number one; lose and there is no second chance. The pressure is great on both teams, and the fans feel it, too.

Very few Super Bowl games have lived up to all of the hype they have received. Only seven of the first 28 games have been settled by a touchdown or less. Most have been blowouts. Yet one-sided final scores haven't dimmed any of the excitement of the event. It's still a "super" way to spend a Sunday in January every year.

How the Super Bowl Was Born

The first Super Bowl was played on January 15, 1967, but the seeds for that game were planted almost eight years earlier. In August 1959, a wealthy Texas oilman named Lamar Hunt was turned down in his attempt to buy a team in the National Football League (NFL). So Hunt convinced several other businessmen to help him form a new football league. By the fall of 1960, the American Football League (AFL) was in business.

The two leagues had an unwritten agreement not to steal each other's veteran players. But there was no rule about signing new players coming out of college. A bidding battle began, and salaries for college stars shot up. In 1965, for example, the New York Jets signed quarterback Joe Namath out of the University of Alabama for the then-unheard-of sum of $400,000 for three years.

Players loved having the two leagues bid for them, but the owners weren't very happy about the inflated salaries. Things nearly reached a crisis point in 1966 when an AFL veteran, placekicker Pete Gogolak of Buffalo, played out his contract and signed a new deal with the NFL's New York Giants. The AFL struck back by offering contracts to several top NFL players. Suddenly, the bidding battle was becoming an expensive, all-out war. Owners in both leagues decided that the best way to avoid financial disaster was to combine the NFL and AFL. Plans for the merger—which would take four years to complete—were drawn up. An important part of the merger plan was the establishment of a championship game between the winners of the two leagues.

The first problem was what to call the new contest. Officially it was known as the AFL-NFL Championship Game, but that name was just too long and dull. One day, Lamar Hunt watched his daughter play with a high-bouncing rubber ball, called a "super ball." He wondered, "Why not call our game the Super *Bowl*?" Owners, players, and fans liked the name, and it stuck.

The first Super Bowl was scheduled for January 15, 1967, exactly two weeks after the AFL and NFL held their league championship contests. It would take place in the huge Los Angeles Coliseum, which could seat nearly 100,000 fans.

Everything seemed to fall into place perfectly for Super Bowl I, especially for Lamar Hunt. On January 1, 1967, his team, the Kansas City Chiefs, won the AFL title and earned the right to meet the Green Bay Packers in the first Super Bowl. The Packers were NFL champs for the fourth time in six years. Because of their added experience, the Packers were heavily favored to beat the Chiefs.

During the next two weeks, sportswriters from all over the world gathered in Los Angeles and wrote hundreds of stories about the upcoming game. It was one of the biggest media blitzes of all time. Fans around the country prepared to spend Super Sunday in front of their television sets. The one mistake that the planners of Super Bowl I made was their choice of the game site. The two leagues just couldn't sell enough tickets to fill the Los

Angeles Coliseum, and more than 30,000 seats remained empty on game day. (The crowd for Super Bowl I—61,946—is the smallest of any Super Bowl so far.) How tough was it to get people to take tickets? Several days before the game, there was a break-in at the Chiefs' office in Kansas City. Office equipment and other valuable items were stolen, but 2,000 Super Bowl tickets were just left behind by the robbers.

The game that the fans in Los Angeles and around the country saw on January 15 wasn't the most exciting football contest of all time—Green Bay won easily, 35–10. But Super Bowl I did make history, and it started one of the most important traditions in sports.

Super Bowl Bests

Two awards are given out every year at the Super Bowl. The winning team is presented with the Vince Lombardi Trophy that goes to the National Football League champion. That trophy is named after the coach who led the Green Bay Packers to victories in Super Bowls I and II. A second trophy is handed out to the game's Most Valuable Player (MVP). You can find a listing of Super Bowl winners and MVPs on pages 12–13.

Suppose some other awards were presented for the most outstanding Super Bowl performances of all time. Here are some nominees for "Super Bowl Best" trophies.

Best Performance by a Quarterback in a Super Bowl

It usually takes an outstanding effort by a team's quarterback to win a Super Bowl, so there have been at least 28 great quarterbacking performances in Super Bowl history. However, three performances stand out above the others. The nominees played in three straight games in the 1980s.

1. **Phil Simms of the New York Giants in Super Bowl XXI**—Simms completed 22 of 25 passes (88 percent)

during the game to lead New York to a 39–20 victory over the Denver Broncos. He also threw for three touchdowns and no interceptions. "I've never played better," Simms said after the game. "Almost every pass landed exactly where I wanted it to."

2. **Doug Williams of the Washington Redskins in Super Bowl XXII**—During the second quarter of his team's game against the Denver Broncos, Williams connected on 9 of 11 passes for 228 yards and four touchdowns. One of those touchdown passes went for a record 80 yards to Ricky Sanders. Williams' play helped turn a 10–0 Denver lead into a 42–10 Washington victory. Amazingly, Williams had not even been the Redskins' starting quarterback when the season began.

3. **Joe Montana of the San Francisco 49ers in Super Bowl XXIII**—Montana engineered the best last-minute drive in the history of the Super Bowl to lead the 49ers to a 20–16 win over the Cincinnati Bengals. With Cincinnati leading 16–13, the 49ers took over on their own 8-yard line with just over three minutes to go in the game. Montana completed 8 of 9 passes. (He said he missed on the one pass because his heart was beating so hard.) His last pass was a 10-yard toss to John Taylor for the winning touchdown.

Best Performance by a Running Back in a Super Bowl

Some running backs use speed to outrun their opponents' defensive players. Others use power to run over possible tacklers. These three nominees could do both:

1. **John Riggins of the Washington Redskins in Super Bowl XVII**—Everybody in the NFL thought that John Riggins was a little crazy. He played one season with a Mohawk haircut, for example. Riggins

was also one of the greatest runners of all time. Against Miami in Super Bowl XVII, he rambled for 166 yards on 38 carries, both records at the time. His finest play occurred in the last period with Miami leading 17–13. The Redskins were facing a fourth down play with one yard to go for the first down. Every Miami defender was playing close to the line of scrimmage. They all knew that Riggins would get the ball and try to bully his way to the first down. Instead, Riggins took the ball, found a small opening to the outside, and outraced the entire Miami defensive team across the goal line to put Washington ahead for good.

2. **Marcus Allen of the Los Angeles Raiders in Super Bowl XVIII**—A year after John Riggins set a record for rushing yardage, Allen broke the record against Riggins' Redskins. He ran over and around Washington defenders for 191 yards on 20 carries, or almost 10 yards a play. He also scored two touchdowns. One went for 74 yards, which is still a Super Bowl record.

3. **Emmitt Smith of the Dallas Cowboys in Super Bowl XXVIII**—Smith's performance against Buffalo turned a close contest into a blowout. He took over the second half of the game, carrying the ball on 15 of 18 plays on two Dallas touchdown drives. Smith finished the contest with 132 yards on 30 carries and those two TDs.

Best Performance by a Receiver in a Super Bowl Game

While running backs need speed and power to be successful, wide receivers need either speed or trickiness. They also have to be able to hang onto the ball even when they are being clobbered by a defender. Here are three such nominees:

1. **Max McGee of the Green Bay Packers in Super Bowl I**—McGee wasn't very fast, and he wasn't even a starter for the Packers. But somehow he had enough skill to play 12 years in the NFL. Against the Kansas City Chiefs, he came off the bench early in the game to score the first touchdown ever in Super Bowl history. It was a tough catch. He had to reach behind him to snare the ball and then slip past all of the Kansas City defenders to reach the end zone.

2. **Lynn Swann of the Pittsburgh Steelers in Super Bowl X**—You can probably figure that someone named Swann would be very graceful, and Lynn Swann was. Against the Dallas Cowboys, he caught four passes for a remarkable 161 yards and two long touchdowns. The last touchdown came late in the game and helped seal Pittsburgh's second consecutive Super Bowl win.

3. **Jerry Rice of the San Francisco 49ers in Super Bowls XXIII and XXIV**—Rice had outstanding games two years in a row. In San Francisco's last-minute victory over Cincinnati, he caught 11 passes for 215 yards, including three in the thrilling final drive, and was named the game's MVP. The next year, he made "only" seven catches for 148 yards, but three of those receptions went for touchdowns. "Jerry Rice is close to being the perfect physical human being," said teammate Randy Cross.

Best Turnaround Performance in a Super Bowl Game

This is a special award that goes to the player who started out having a terrible game but wound up being a hero. It goes to:

1. **Placekicker Jim O'Brien of the Baltimore Colts in Super Bowl V**—O'Brien was a rookie during the 1971

season, and he made lots of beginner's mistakes during the year. He made fewer than half of his field-goal attempts. In the Super Bowl against Dallas, he started off with two flubs. He missed his first extra-point attempt and his first field-goal try. Had he connected on either kick, the Colts would not have been tied with Dallas with just a few seconds remaining in the game. O'Brien turned from goat to hero when he kicked a 32-yard field goal to make Baltimore a winner.

Here are a few other suggestions for "Super Bowl Bests" that you can read about in this book:

Best Ending to a Game—Check out Super Bowls V, XIII, XXIII, and XXV.

Funniest Moment in a Game—Read about Super Bowl VII.

Best Performance by an Underdog Team—See Super Bowl III.

Best Performance by a Favored Team—See Super Bowl XX.

Longest Winning Streak by a Conference—Look up Super Bowls XIX-XXVIII.

Super Bowl Fast Facts

Here are 15 facts about the first 28 Super Bowl games. Find out how many your friends know. You'll learn lots more as you read this book.

1. The Dallas Cowboys have played in the most Super Bowls—seven.
2. Joe Montana has not thrown a single interception in four Super Bowl appearances.
3. Preston Pearson is the only person to play for three different teams (Baltimore, Pittsburgh, and Dallas).
4. Don Shula is the only person who has coached two different teams in a Super Bowl (Baltimore and Miami).
5. The Green Bay Packers won the first two Super Bowls but have not appeared in another game since.
6. The Pittsburgh Steelers won three games played in the 1970s, and the San Francisco 49ers won three games played in the 1980s.
7. Chuck Howley of Dallas is the only player from a losing team to be named Most Valuable Player (Super Bowl V).
8. Joe Montana has been named Most Valuable Player three times.

11

9. Five teams have appeared in only one Super Bowl each: Chicago Bears, Los Angeles Rams, New England Patriots, New York Jets, and Philadelphia Eagles. The Jets and Bears won; the other three teams lost.

10. National Football Conference (NFC) teams have won the last ten Super Bowls in a row.

11. The last American Football Conference (AFC) team to win a Super Bowl was the Los Angeles Raiders (Super Bowl XVIII).

12. The Washington Redskins scored 35 points in a single quarter in Super Bowl XXII.

13. No Super Bowl team has ever fallen behind by more than ten points and come back to win the game.

14. The most points both teams have scored in a game is 69 (XXVII); the fewest points both teams have scored in a game is 21 (VII).

15. Max McGee scored the first touchdown in Super Bowl I; Emmitt Smith scored the last touchdown in Super Bowl XXVIII.

Games I-XXVIII at a Glance

Game	Winner	Loser	MVP
I	Green Bay 35	Kansas City 10	Bart Starr
II	Green Bay 33	Oakland 14	Bart Starr
III	New York Jets 16	Baltimore 7	Joe Namath
IV	Kansas City 23	Minnesota 7	Len Dawson
V	Baltimore 16	Dallas 13	Chuck Howley
VI	Dallas 24	Miami 3	Roger Staubach
VII	Miami 14	Washington 7	Jake Scott
VIII	Miami 24	Minnesota 7	Larry Csonka
IX	Pittsburgh 16	Minnesota 6	Franco Harris
X	Pittsburgh 21	Dallas 17	Lynn Swann
XI	Oakland 32	Minnesota 14	Fred Biletnikoff
XII	Dallas 27	Denver 10	Harvey Martin/

			Randy White
XIII	Pittsburgh 35	Dallas 31	Terry Bradshaw
XIV	Pittsburgh 31	L.A. Rams 19	Terry Bradshaw
XV	Oakland 27	Philadelphia 10	Jim Plunkett
XVI	San Francisco 26	Cincinnati 21	Joe Montana
XVII	Washington 27	Miami 17	John Riggins
XVIII	L.A. Raiders 38	Washington 9	Marcus Allen
XIX	San Francisco 38	Miami 16	Joe Montana
XX	Chicago 46	New England 10	Richard Dent
XXI	N.Y. Giants 39	Denver 20	Phil Simms
XXII	Washington 42	Denver 10	Doug Williams
XXIII	San Francisco 20	Cincinnati 16	Jerry Rice
XXIV	San Francisco 55	Denver 10	Joe Montana
XXV	N.Y. Giants 20	Buffalo 19	Ottis Anderson
XXVI	Washington 37	Buffalo 24	Mark Rypien
XXVII	Dallas 52	Buffalo 17	Troy Aikman
XXVIII	Dallas 30	Buffalo 13	Emmitt Smith

Super Bowl Game Summaries

Super Bowl I—The Pack Attacks
January 15, 1967—Los Angeles, California

Everyone except the most loyal AFL fans expected the NFL champion Green Bay Packers to wallop the Kansas City Chiefs of the AFL in Super Bowl I. The Packers were used to winning titles. Under their legendary coach Vince Lombardi, the Pack had already played in five NFL championship games in the 1960s and had won four.

The Chiefs were younger and faster than the Packers but were no match for Green Bay's power on offense or defense. The Packers would usually wear down opponents with a punishing ground game led by fullback Jim Taylor and halfback Elijah Pitts. Green Bay quarterback Bart Starr was also a master at picking apart defenses with pinpoint passes.

Kansas City's offense revolved around quarterback Len Dawson and speedy receivers such as Otis Taylor and Chris Burford. But would Dawson have enough time to get off his passes against the hard-rushing Packer defense?

As it turned out, Super Bowl I had an unlikely hero. He was a 12-year veteran pass receiver for the Packers named Max McGee. McGee had played very little during the regular season. He didn't expect to play in the Super Bowl either and had snuck out of his hotel room the night before and stayed out very late. McGee planned to relax on the bench during the game. But on the second play, Packer pass receiver Boyd Dowler was injured, and Lombardi yelled, "McGee, get in there."

"At first I thought he was just yelling at me for not paying attention," McGee said. Then he realized he was not going to be resting this day.

A few moments later, Bart Starr faked a short pass, then spotted McGee racing across the middle of the field, and threw to him. The ball was a little behind Max, but he reached back, grabbed it with one hand, and outraced a Chiefs defender across the goal line for the first touchdown in Super Bowl history.

Kansas City came back in the second quarter to tie the game, 7–7. The game stayed close, and by halftime Green Bay held only a 14–10 lead. The Packers dominated the second half, however, outscoring the Chiefs 21–0 for a 35–10 triumph. McGee caught seven passes during the game and scored two touchdowns, one more than he had tallied during the entire season. For his outstanding leadership, Starr was named Most Valuable Player of Super Bowl I.

After the game, Coach Lombardi told friends that he was just happy to have won the game and successfully defended the honor of the NFL.

Key Play: Starr's pass to McGee for the first touchdown was key, but Kansas City coach Hank Stram felt a more important play occurred at the beginning of the second half. The Chiefs were driving for a go-ahead touchdown when Packer Willie Wood intercepted a Len Dawson pass and ran it back 50 yards. Elijah Pitts scored on the next play to put Green Bay ahead 21–10.

15

Statistics of Super Bowl I

SCORE BY PERIODS

Kansas City Chiefs (AFL)	0	10	0	0—10
Green Bay Packers (NFL)	7	7	14	7—35

SCORING

Green Bay—McGee 37 pass from Starr (Chandler kick)

Kansas City—McClinton 7 pass from Dawson (Mercer kick)

Green Bay—J. Taylor 14 run (Chandler kick)

Kansas City—Mercer field goal (31)

Green Bay—Pitts 5 run (Chandler kick)

Green Bay—McGee 13 pass from Starr (Chandler kick)

Green Bay—Pitts 1 run (Chandler kick)

KEY TEAM STATISTICS

	Kansas City	Green Bay
Yards gained rushing	72	130
Yards gained passing	167	228
Total yards gained	239	358
Interceptions thrown	1	1
Fumbles lost	0	0
Total turnovers	1	1
Number of times sacked	6	3
Yardage lost via sacks	61	22

KEY INDIVIDUAL STATISTICS*

Kansas City

Leading Passer:	Dawson	16–27, 211 yards, 1 TD, 1 int.
Leading Rusher:	Dawson	3 carries for 24 yards
Leading Receivers:	Burford	4 for 67 yards
	Taylor	4 for 57 yards
Defensive Leader:	Mitchell	1 int.

16

| Kicker: | Mercer | 1–1 PAT, 1–2 field goals |

Green Bay

Leading Passer:	Starr	16–23, 250 yards, 2 TD, 1 int.
Leading Rushers:	J. Taylor	16 carries for 53 yards, 1 TD
	Pitts	11 carries for 45 yards, 2 TD
Leading Receiver:	McGee	7 for 138 yards, 2 TD
Defensive Leader:	Wood	1 int. (50 yards)
Kicker:	Chandler	5–5 PAT, 0–0 field goals

* Statistics abbreviations:
  TD = touchdown; int. = interception; PAT = point after touchdown

Super Bowl II—The Pack Is Back
January 14, 1968—Miami, Florida

Vince Lombardi's Green Bay Packers were back in Super Bowl II to defend their title. But they almost didn't make it there. The Packers barely edged out the Dallas Cowboys in the closing seconds of the NFL championship game. The Wisconsin weather was so cold that the game became known as the "Ice Bowl."

The AFL's Oakland Raiders had much less trouble earning a spot in the Super Bowl. Oakland breezed to a 13–1 record during the season and routed Houston 40–7 to win the league title. The Raiders had a solid offense led by quarterback Daryle Lamonica, and their defensive unit was known for hard hitting.

When the two teams squared off in Miami's Orange Bowl, there was some added drama. Rumors spread that Lombardi planned to retire after the big game. The Packers' coach wouldn't confirm the rumors, but he told

17

his team in a pregame pep talk, "All the glory, everything that you've had, everything that you've won is going to be small in comparison to winning this one. Boys, I tell you, I'd be so proud of that."

The pep talk worked. Green Bay won the coin toss, received the opening kickoff, and moved steadily down the field. The drive ended with a 39-yard field goal by place-kicker Don Chandler. The Packers continued to control the ball in the first half and went into the locker room leading 16–7. The big plays were three field goals by Chandler and a long touchdown pass from Bart Starr to Boyd Dowler.

Green Bay dominated the Raiders in the second half as well. The Pack tallied ten points in the third period and added a fourth-quarter TD on a long Herb Adderley pass interception before Oakland could get onto the score-board again. The final score of 33–14 marked a second straight rout by the NFL.

Oakland coach Johnny Rauch summed up his team's feelings when he said, "It's tough to accept a beating, especially when you're not used to it."

Key play: The 62-yard touchdown pass from Starr to Dowler was made possible by poor pass coverage by the Raiders' defensive backs. That score broke the game open in the second period.

Statistics of Super Bowl II

SCORE BY PERIODS

Oakland Raiders (AFL)	0	7	0	7—14
Green Bay Packers (NFL)	3	13	10	7—33

SCORING
Green Bay—Chandler field goal (39)
Green Bay—Chandler field goal (20)
Green Bay—Dowler 62 pass from Starr (Chandler kick)

Oakland—Miller 23 pass from Lamonica (Blanda kick)
Green Bay—Chandler field goal (43)
Green Bay—Anderson 2 run (Chandler kick)
Green Bay—Chandler field goal (31)
Green Bay—Adderley 60 int. (Chandler kick)
Oakland —Miller 23 pass from Lamonica (Blanda kick)

KEY TEAM STATISTICS

	Oakland	Green Bay
Yards gained rushing	107	160
Yards gained passing	186	162
Total yards gained	293	322
Interceptions thrown	1	0
Fumbles lost	2	0
Total turnovers	3	0
Number of times sacked	3	4
Yardage lost via sacks	40	22

KEY INDIVIDUAL STATISTICS

Oakland

Leading Passer:	Lamonica	15–34, 208 yards, 2 TD, 1 int.
Leading Rusher:	Dixon	12 carries for 54 yards
Leading Receiver:	Miller	5 for 84 yards, 2 TD
Kicker:	Blanda	2–2 PAT, 0–1 field goals

Green Bay

Leading Passer:	Starr	13–24, 202 yards, 1 TD, 0 int.
Leading Rushers:	Wilson	17 carries for 62 yards
	Anderson	14 carries for 48 yards, 1 TD
Leading Receivers:	Dale	4 for 43 yards
	Fleming	4 for 35 yards
Defensive Leader:	Adderley	1 int. (60 yards, TD)
Kicker:	Chandler	3–3 PAT, 4–4 field goals

Super Bowl III— Namath Keeps His Word
January 12, 1969—Miami, Florida

Before Super Bowl III, NFL fans often made fun of the AFL and called it a "minor league." They soon stopped their bragging, however.

Super Bowl III featured the NFL's high-scoring Baltimore Colts, who had put together a 15–1 record, against a young, cocky New York Jets AFL club. The Jets were 19-point underdogs, but some writers predicted Baltimore would win by as much as 45 points.

The Jets' leader was 25-year-old quarterback Joe Namath. His nickname was "Broadway Joe," because he liked to go out to nightclubs on New York's Broadway. He also liked to brag. Three days before Super Bowl III, Namath shocked the press by saying, "We're going to win Sunday. In fact, I guarantee it!"

The Jets showed right away that they weren't afraid of the Colts. On the third play of the game, Jets fullback Matt Snell crashed into a Colt tackler so hard that the defender had to be helped off the field. Then, led by Namath's crisp passes and Snell's bruising running, the Jets marched to a second quarter touchdown for a 7–0 lead. It was the first time an AFL club had ever led in a Super Bowl.

Nothing went right for the Colts all afternoon. They missed two short field goals and had several passes intercepted deep in Jet territory. Just before halftime, Baltimore tried a trick play. Quarterback Earl Morrall handed off to running back Tom Matte, who lateraled back to Morrall to make a long pass. Baltimore end Jimmy Orr was wide open on the Jets' 10-yard line and called for the ball, but Morrall never saw him. Instead, he threw an incomplete pass to another Colts player.

By the time Baltimore scored its first touchdown late in the game, New York was already ahead by 16 points. The 16–7 Jets victory shocked the football world. More important, the AFL proved that it was finally equal to the NFL. After all, Joe Namath had guaranteed it.

Key play: A Randy Beverly interception in the Jets' end zone at the end of the first quarter stopped the Colts from scoring first in the game and started New York on its own scoring drive.

Statistics of Super Bowl III

SCORE BY PERIODS

New York Jets (AFL)	0	7	6	3—16
Baltimore Colts (NFL)	0	0	0	7— 7

SCORING
New York—Snell 4 run (Turner kick)
New York—Turner field goal (32)
New York—Turner field goal (30)
New York—Turner field goal (9)
Baltimore—Hill 1 run (Michaels kick)

KEY TEAM STATISTICS

	New York	Baltimore
Yards gained rushing	142	143
Yards gained passing	195	181
Total yards gained	337	324
Interceptions thrown	0	4
Fumbles lost	1	1
Total turnovers	1	5
Number of times sacked	2	0
Yardage lost via sacks	11	0

KEY INDIVIDUAL STATISTICS
New York

Leading Passer:	Namath	17–28, 206 yards, 0 TD, 0 int.
Leading Rusher:	Snell	30 carries for 121 yards, 1 TD
Leading Receiver:	Sauer	8 for 133 yards
Defensive Leader:	Beverly	2 int.
Kicker:	Turner	1–1 PAT, 3–5 field goals

Baltimore

Leading Passers:	Unitas	11–24, 110 yards, 0 TD, 1 int.
	Morrall	6–17, 71 yards, 0 TD, 3 int.
Leading Rusher:	Matte	11 carries for 116 yards
Leading Receiver:	Richardson	6 for 58 yards
Kicker:	Michaels	1–1 PAT, 0–2 field goals

Super Bowl IV—Kansas City Strikes Back

January 11, 1970—New Orleans, Louisiana

Two things made Super Bowl IV special. First, it would be the last game between champions of two separate leagues. Before the next season, the AFL and NFL would complete their merger and become one body. Second, an AFL victory would put the two leagues dead even at 2–2 in Super Bowl wins. The AFL Kansas City Chiefs had another thought in mind as they prepared for the big game. They wanted to avenge their loss in Super Bowl I three years before. Their NFL opponents were the Minnesota Vikings, who featured the mighty "Purple People Eaters" on defense and an offense led by a gutsy, scrambling quarterback named Joe Kapp. The Chiefs had no fancy nicknames, but their defense was outstanding, and their offense was explosive. Offensive stars included quarterback Len Dawson, receiver Otis Taylor, and running back Mike Garrett.

The NFL club was heavily favored to win by football writers—just as in Super Bowl III. And, once again, the "experts" were proved wrong. Dawson engineered three drives deep into Viking territory during the first half. Each time, the Purple People Eaters stalled the Chiefs, but they couldn't stop placekicker Jan Stenerud. He kicked three field goals to put Kansas City up 9–0. Then a big Minnesota turnover led to a KC touchdown before halftime, and the Chiefs went into the locker room up 16–0.

Minnesota was able to mount only one successful offensive drive in the second half to pull to within 16–7. But the Chiefs quickly matched that score when Otis Taylor caught a short pass from Dawson, faked out his defender, and raced for a 46-yard touchdown. That made the score 23–7, which was how it ended.

After the game, Kapp gave a lot of credit to the Chiefs' defensive line. "They resembled a redwood forest out there today," he said.

Key play: Late in the second quarter, Minnesota's Charlie West fumbled a kickoff on his own 19-yard line with the score 9–0. A few plays later, Mike Garrett raced in for a 5-yard TD to give the Chiefs a commanding halftime lead.

Statistics of Super Bowl IV

SCORE BY PERIODS

Kansas City Chiefs (AFL)	3	13	7	0—23
Minnesota Vikings (NFL)	0	0	7	0— 7

SCORING

Kansas City—Stenerud field goal (48)
Kansas City—Stenerud field goal (32)
Kansas City—Stenerud field goal (25)

Kansas City—Garrett 5 run (Stenerud kick)
Minnesota—Osborn 4 run (Cox kick)
Kansas City—Taylor 46 pass from Dawson (Stenerud kick)

KEY TEAM STATISTICS

	Kansas City	Minnesota
Yards gained rushing	151	67
Yards gained passing	122	172
Total yards gained	273	239
Interceptions thrown	1	3
Fumbles lost	0	2
Total turnovers	1	5
Number of times sacked	3	3
Yardage lost via sacks	20	27

KEY INDIVIDUAL STATISTICS
Kansas City

Leading Passer:	Dawson	12–17, 142 yards, 1 TD, 1 int.
Leading Rusher:	Garrett	11 carries for 39 yards, 1 TD
Leading Receiver:	Taylor	6 for 81 yards, 1 TD
Defensive Leader:	Robinson	1 int., 1 fumble recovery
Kicker:	Stenerud	2–2 PAT, 3–3 field goals

Minnesota

Leading Passer:	Kapp	16–25, 183 yards, 0 TD, 2 int.
Leading Rusher:	Brown	6 carries for 26 yards
Leading Receiver:	Henderson	7 for 111 yards
Defensive Leader:	Krause	1 int.
Kicker:	Cox	1–1 PAT, 0–1 field goals

Super Bowl V—The "Blooper Bowl"

January 17, 1971—Miami, Florida

The first four Super Bowls had been pretty exciting, but none of them had been close. Football fans were ready for a "super" ending, and they got that in Super Bowl V. They also got to see one of the sloppiest championship football games of all time.

Before the 1970 season, the AFL and NFL merged to form one league with two conferences. The ten AFL teams and three of the 16 NFL teams—the Baltimore Colts, Cleveland Browns, and Pittsburgh Steelers—were grouped into the American Football Conference. The remaining 13 NFL teams became the National Football Conference.

The Colts ran up an impressive 11–2–1 record in their first year in the AFC and earned a spot in Super Bowl V. Their NFC opponents were the Dallas Cowboys. Both teams had added reasons for wanting to win the big game. Baltimore hoped to prove its loss to the Jets in Super Bowl III had been a fluke. Dallas, which had come close to beating Green Bay to qualify for Super Bowls I and II, wanted to show it wasn't "second best" anymore.

Maybe the added pressure to win made both clubs a little tight as the game began. In any case, nothing seemed to go right. There were four fumbles and six interceptions during the game and lots of penalties and mental mistakes as well.

Baltimore errors in the first half allowed the Cowboys to move close to the Baltimore goal line twice, but Dallas mistakes each time forced them to settle for field goals instead of touchdowns. Baltimore finally made a touchdown on a long deflected pass from Unitas to John Mackey in the second period, but kicker Jim O'Brien missed the point after touchdown, and the score remained 6–6.

With less than two minutes to go in the game, the score was still tied—at 13–13. Would this be the first Super Bowl to go into overtime?

Dallas got the ball on the Baltimore 48-yard line, ready to drive for the winning score. The Cowboys lost yardage on two running plays and also were called for a penalty. Dallas quarterback Craig Morton needed a long pass completion to set up a field goal. But as Morton's pass sailed downfield, Baltimore's Mike Curtis cut inside of Dallas receiver Dan Reeves, intercepted and ran the ball to the Dallas 28-yard line. There were only nine seconds to go when O'Brien came onto the field to attempt a winning Baltimore field goal.

The Colt rookie was a little nervous. He had already missed an extra point and field goal attempt in the game. Dallas called a timeout to build up the pressure, but that strategy didn't work. O'Brien's kick started out a little to the right, then straightened out and sailed directly through the goalposts as time ran out. At last, the Colts were Super Bowl champs.

Key play: When Baltimore's Jim Duncan fumbled the second-half kickoff, Dallas was in good position to put the game out of reach. However, Dallas running back Duane Thomas's fumble on the Colt 2-yard line ended the Cowboy drive and kept Baltimore alive.

Statistics of Super Bowl V

SCORE BY PERIODS

Baltimore Colts (AFC)	0	6	0	10—16
Dallas Cowboys (NFC)	3	10	0	0—13

SCORING
Dallas—Clark field goal (14)
Dallas—Clark field goal (30)
Baltimore—Mackey 75 pass from Unitas (kick failed)
Dallas—Thomas 7 pass from Unitas (Clark kick)

Baltimore—Nowatzke 2 run (O'Brien kick)
Baltimore—O'Brien field goal (32)

KEY TEAM STATISTICS

	Baltimore	Dallas
Yards gained rushing	69	102
Yards gained passing	260	113
Total yards gained	329	215
Interceptions thrown	3	3
Fumbles lost	3	1
Total turnovers	6	4
Number of times sacked	0	2
Yardage lost via sacks	0	14

KEY INDIVIDUAL STATISTICS

Baltimore

Leading Passers:	Morrall	7–15, 147 yards, 0 TD, 1 int.
	Unitas	3–9, 88 yards, 1 TD, 2 int.
Leading Rusher:	Nowatzke	10 carries for 33 yards, 1 TD
Leading Receivers:	Jefferson	3 for 52 yards
	Mackey	2 for 80 yards, 1 TD
Defensive Leader:	Volk	1 int. for 30 yards
Kicker:	O'Brien	1–2 PAT, 1–2 field goals

Dallas

Leading Passer:	Morton	12–26, 127 yards, 1 TD, 3 int.
Leading Rushers:	Garrison	12 carries for 65 yards
	Thomas	18 carries for 35 yards
Leading Receiver:	Reeves	5 for 46 yards
Defensive Leader:	Howley	2 int. for 22 yards
Kicker:	Clark	1–1 PAT, 2–2 field goals

Super Bowl VI—Dallas Does It

January 16, 1972—New Orleans, Louisiana

The Dallas Cowboys didn't let memories of their last-second loss in Super Bowl V affect them as they systematically took apart the Miami Dolphins in Super Bowl VI. Dallas dominated nearly every part of the game. Running backs Duane Thomas, Walt Garrison, and Calvin Hill pounded into the Miami line time after time to set a new Super Bowl record with 252 yards rushing. Cowboy quarterback Roger Staubach also had an error-free game, connecting on 12 of 19 passes for two touchdowns and no interceptions. Meanwhile, the Dallas defense held Miami to under 200 yards in total offense. That established a Super Bowl record that stood for several years.

One interesting sidelight of the game was the much-discussed telephone call from President Richard Nixon to Miami coach Don Shula suggesting a pass play to try in the game (see page 3). Dallas was ready for that play, and Paul Warfield never came close to making a big catch in the game.

When the final gun sounded in Tulane Stadium in New Orleans, the Cowboys were Super Bowl champs at last, with a 24–3 drubbing of Miami.

Key play: Early in the game, Dolphins fullback Larry Csonka fumbled for the first time all season. His mistake ended a strong Miami drive and set up the Cowboys for their first score of the game.

Statistics of Super Bowl VI

SCORE BY PERIODS

Miami Dolphins (AFC)	0	3	0	0— 3
Dallas Cowboys (NFC)	3	7	7	7—24

SCORING

Dallas—Clark field goal (9)

Dallas—Alworth 7 pass from Staubach (Clark kick)
Miami—Yepremian field goal (31)
Dallas—D. Thomas 3 run (Clark kick)
Dallas—Ditka 7 pass from Staubach (Clark kick)

KEY TEAM STATISTICS

	Miami	Dallas
Yards gained rushing	80	252
Yards gained passing	105	100
Total yards gained	185	352
Interceptions thrown	1	0
Fumbles lost	2	1
Total turnovers	3	1
Number of times sacked	1	2
Yardage lost via sacks	29	19

KEY INDIVIDUAL STATISTICS

Miami

Leading Passer:	Griese	12–23, 134 yards, 0 TD, 1 int.
Leading Rushers:	Csonka	9 carries for 40 yards
	Kiick	10 carries for 40 yards
Leading Receiver:	Warfield	4 for 39 yards
Kicker:	Yepremian	0–0 PAT, 1–2 field goals

Dallas

Leading Passer:	Staubach	12–19, 119 yards, 2 TD, 0 int.
Leading Rusher:	D. Thomas	19 carries for 95 yards, 1 TD
Leading Receivers:	Alworth	2 for 28 yards, 1 TD
	Ditka	2 for 28 yards, 1 TD
Defensive Leader:	Howley	1 int. (41 yards), 1 fumble recovery
Kicker:	Clark	3–3 PAT, 1–1 field goals

Super Bowl VII—A Perfect Ending

January 14, 1973—Los Angeles, California

Super Bowl VII was held at the Los Angeles Coliseum, the same place as Super Bowl I. There was a big difference this time, however. The Super Bowl was now a big hit, and the huge stadium was packed. Another difference was that most fans believed the AFC team could win in Super VII.

The AFC champs were the Miami Dolphins for a second straight year. The Dolphins had not lost a game all season, finishing with a perfect 16–0 record. There was a lot of pressure on the Dolphins and their coach. In the NFL's 53-year history, no NFL team had ever completed a season with all wins. Also, Coach Shula's teams had lost in both Super Bowls III and VI, and he hoped to change his luck.

The Dolphins and their opponents, the Washington Redskins, seemed tight throughout most of the game, and the contest was pretty dull—until the last two minutes. With 2:07 left, Miami was up 14–0. The Dolphins set up for a field goal that would put the game totally out of reach of the Redskins. The tiny (5' 8") Miami placekicker Garo Yepremian booted the ball, but a huge Washington lineman blocked the kick, and the ball went rolling back toward Yepremian. All Garo had to do was to fall on the ball, but he picked it up instead and tried to throw to a teammate. The ball was deflected and Washington's Mike Bass grabbed it and raced 49 yards for a touchdown to make the score 14–7. Things were pretty tense on the Miami sidelines. Dolphins fullback Larry Csonka tried to motivate his teammates. "Come on, guys. This is what we've been waiting for for two years," he shouted.

The Dolphins' offense used up most of the remaining time, and the defense held Washington scoreless to end the game. Afterwards, Coach Shula breathed a sigh of relief as he was carried off the field on his players'

"Broadway Joe" Namath guaranteed a New York Jets victory in
Super Bowl III. Here, Baltimore's Bubba Smith tried in vain to block
Namath's pass, but the Jets' star delivered both the pass and the win.

This is the quick slant pass play that President Richard Nixon suggested to Miami Dolphins coach Don Shula prior to Super Bowl VI. Miami's Bob Griese connected with Paul Warfield, but the Cowboys still sank the Dolphins, 24–3.

The Dolphins' placekicker, Garo Yepremian, muffed a field goal attempt in Super Bowl VII, then tried to pick up the ball and pass it. *(below)* Mike Bass (41) of the Redskins grabbed the ball and ran for a TD. Luckily, this Super Bowl blooper did not cost the Dolphins the game.

Larry Csonka, the Dolphins'
running back was the MVP
in Super Bowl VIII.

One big reason the Pittsburgh Steelers were a perennial Super Bowl power was running back Franco Harris, shown here racing into the end zone in Super Bowl IX.

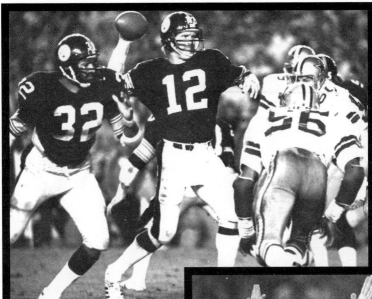

Pittsburgh Steelers quarterback Terry Bradshaw fired four TD passes in Super Bowl XIII. *(above)*

Touchdown! San Francisco 49ers quarterback Joe Montana signals score in Super Bowl XVI. Montana has more Super Bowl TD passes than any other quarterback. *(right)*

Graceful as a swan, Steelers receiver Lynn Swann grabbed four passes for 161 yards in Super Bowl X. Swann's acrobatic catches were often unbelievable. *(left)*

John Riggins of the Washington Redskins was unstoppable in Super Bowl XVII, rushing for a record 166 yards. (above)

A year later, Raiders running back Marcus Allen broke Riggins' record by running for 191 yards in Super Bowl XVIII.

Dolphins quarterback Dan Marino passed for 318 yards in Super Bowl XIX but couldn't beat Joe Montana and the San Francisco 49ers.

49ers running back Roger Craig spikes the ball after his second touchdown in Super Bowl XIX.

Chicago Bears quarterback Jim McMahon dives over the goal line in Super Bowl XX. The Bears crushed the Patriots 46–10.

New York Giants quarterback Phil Simms was sensational in Super Bowl XXI. *(left)*

The New York Giants' awesome defense celebrates a safety-producing sack of Denver Broncos quarterback John Elway in Super Bowl XXI.

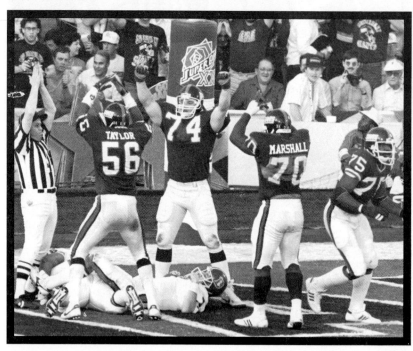

The amazing Jerry Rice, receiver for the San Francisco 49ers, celebrates one of his three TD pass receptions in Super Bowl XXIV.

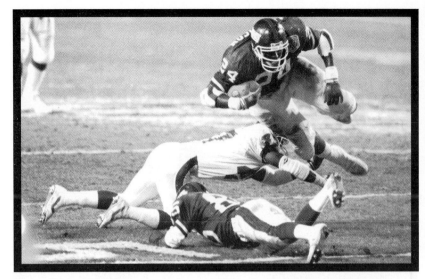

Ottis Anderson leaps over the goal line in Super Bowl XXV to score a decisive fourth-quarter touchdown for the New York Giants.

The New York Giants won Super Bowl XXV, but Buffalo's Thurman Thomas gave them a run for their money. Thomas races for one of his four career Super Bowl TDs here.

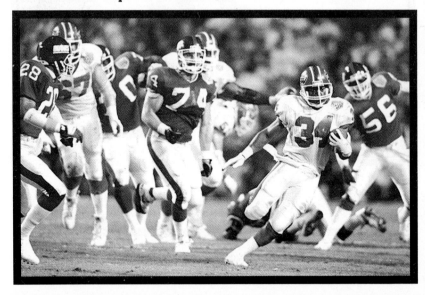

The Buffalo Bills would have beaten New York in Super Bowl XXV, but Bills kicker Scott Norwood missed on this field goal attempt in the final play of the game. The Giants won 20–19.

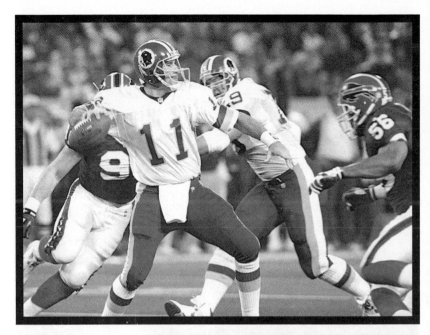

Washington Redskins quarterback Mark Rypien winds up and lets go one of his 18 completions in Super Bowl XXVI.

One of Washington quarterback Mark Rypien's favorite targets was receiver Art Monk who caught five passes in Washington's first drive in Super Bowl XXVI.

Dallas Cowboys QB Troy Aikman goes airborne as he scrambles for yardage in Super Bowl XXVII. The Cowboys completely clobbered the Bills, and Aikman was named the game's MVP.

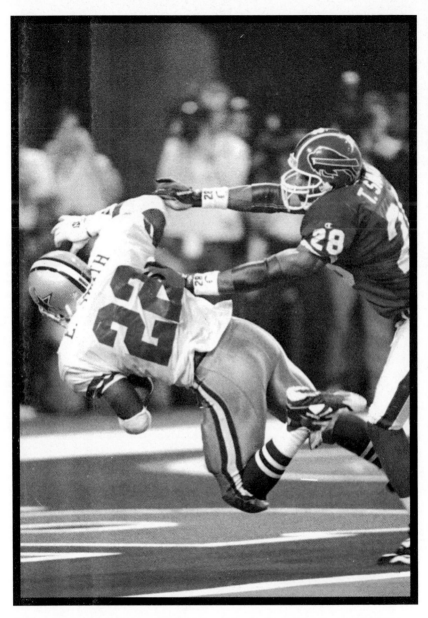

"Get me the ball," Emmitt Smith of the Dallas Cowboys told his coaches in Super Bowl XXVIII. He did, ran for 132 yards and 2 TDs, and won the MVP award for the game.

shoulders. "I was aware of the reputation I had gotten. The losses were there in my mind. But that's all in the past now," he said.

Key play: The game was primarily a defensive struggle until the closing seconds of the first period when Miami pass receiver Howard Twilley beat Redskins defender Pat Fischer to the outside and scored on a 28-yard pass from Bob Griese.

Statistics of Super Bowl VII

SCORE BY PERIODS

Miami Dolphins (AFC)	7	7	0	0—14
Washington Redskins (NFC)	0	0	0	7— 7

SCORING
Miami—Twilley 28 pass from Griese (Yepremian kick)
Miami—Kiick 1 run (Yepremian kick)
Washington—Bass 49 fumble return (Knight kick)

KEY TEAM STATISTICS

	Miami	Washington
Yards gained rushing	184	141
Yards gained passing	69	87
Total yards gained	253	228
Interceptions thrown	1	3
Fumbles lost	1	0
Total turnovers	2	3
Number of times sacked	2	2
Yardage lost via sacks	17	19

KEY INDIVIDUAL STATISTICS
Miami

Leading Passer:	Griese	8–11, 88 yards, 1 TD, 1 int.
Leading Rusher:	Csonka	15 carries for 112 yards
Leading Receiver:	Warfield	3 for 36 yards
Defensive Leader:	Scott	2 int. (63 yards)
Kicker:	Yepremian	2–2 PAT, 0–1 field goals

Washington

Leading Passer:	Kilmer	14–28, 104 yards, 0 TD, 3 int.
Leading Rusher:	Brown	22 carries for 72 yards
Leading Receiver:	Jefferson	5 for 50 yards
Defensive leader:	Bass	1 fumble recovery (41 yards, TD)
Kicker:	Knight	1–1 PAT, 0–1 field goals

Super Bowl VIII— Dolphin Double Dynamite
January 13, 1974—Houston, Texas

The Miami Dolphins didn't continue to be perfect during the 1973 season, but they did play a nearly perfect game in Super Bowl VIII against the Minnesota Vikings. Miami's hero for the afternoon was hard-running fullback Larry Csonka. Csonka crashed through Minnesota tacklers during Miami's first two offensive drives of the game to help put the Dolphins up quickly, 14–0. Before the end of the day, Csonka would set a Super Bowl record with 145 yards rushing and score two touchdowns.

Once the offense opened up the 14–0 lead, the Miami defense took over. Dolphin defenders plagued Minnesota quarterback Fran Tarkenton all afternoon. He completed 18 of 28 passes but never brought the Vikings close to the goal line until the closing minutes of the game.

With their 24–7 victory, the Dolphins matched the Packers as the only other team to win two consecutive Super Bowls.

Key play: No one Miami play had special importance during the game, but a Minnesota mistake nearly broke the Vikings' spirits. On the opening kickoff of the second half, Minny's John Gilliam made an exciting 65-yard runback to give the Vikings great field position. However, the play was called back because of a clipping penalty, and the Vikings' momentum was halted.

Statistics of Super Bowl VIII

SCORE BY PERIODS

Miami Dolphins (AFC)	14	3	7	0—24
Minnesota Vikings (NFC)	0	0	0	7— 7

SCORING

Miami—Csonka 5 run (Yepremian kick)
Miami—Kiick 1 run (Yepremian kick)
Miami—Yepremian field goal (28)
Miami—Csonka 2 run (Yepremian kick)
Minnesota—Tarkenton 4 run (Cox kick)

KEY TEAM STATISTICS

	Miami	Minnesota
Yards gained rushing	196	72
Yards gained passing	63	166
Total yards gained	259	238
Interceptions thrown	0	1
Fumbles lost	0	1
Total turnovers	0	2
Number of times sacked	1	2
Yardage lost via sacks	10	16

KEY INDIVIDUAL STATISTICS
Miami

Leading Passer:	Griese	6–7, 73 yards, 0 TD, 0 int.
Leading Rusher:	Csonka	33 carries for 145 yards, 2 TD
Leading Receiver:	Warfield	2 for 33 yards
Defensive Leader:	Johnson	1 int. (10 yards)
Kicker:	Yepremian	3–3 PAT, 1–1 field goals

Minnesota

Leading Passer:	Tarkenton	18–28, 182 yards, 0 TD, 1 int.
Leading Rusher:	Reed	11 carries for 32 yards
Leading Receiver:	Foreman	5 for 27 yards
Defensive Leader:	Krause	1 int.
Kicker:	Cox	1–1 PAT, 0–0 field goals

Super Bowl IX—The Men of Steel
January 12, 1975—New Orleans, Louisiana

For the first time in four years, the AFC had a new representative in Super Bowl IX—the Pittsburgh Steelers. The Steelers had been part of the National Football League for 42 years and had never before won a championship or played in a championship game. Their opponents were the Minnesota Vikings, back for their third Super Bowl and eager for their first victory.

Steelers coach Chuck Noll had put together a powerful squad. Quarterback and team leader Terry Bradshaw was so strong he could throw a ball 70 yards in the air. He was backed up on offense by running backs Franco Harris and Rocky Bleier and two superb rookie receivers, Lynn Swann and John Stallworth. The Pittsburgh defensive unit was called the "Steel Curtain" because it was almost impossible for other teams to penetrate it and score. Its stars included linebacker Jack Lambert, cornerback Mel Blount, and a defensive tackle with the scary nickname "Mean Joe" Greene.

Most fans expected a tight defensive struggle in Super Bowl IX between the Steel Curtain and Minnesota's Purple People Eaters. They got what they expected. Neither team was able to score on offense during the first half, and the only points came on a safety when Vikings quarterback Fran Tarkenton fell on a fumble in his own end zone.

In the second half, Franco Harris broke loose for several big runs, including a touchdown that put Pittsburgh up 9–0. Harris ended with a record 158 yards on the ground.

Minnesota made the game exciting early in the fourth period when Terry Brown recovered a blocked punt to cut the lead to 9–6. But that was all the scoring the Vikings could muster. When the game ended, Minnesota had not only lost, 16–6, but had racked up only 119 yards in total offense. That's a record for futility that still stands.

Key play: Late in the first half, Tarkenton found receiver John Gilliam over the middle at the Pittsburgh 5-yard line. Gilliam was hit hard by Steeler safety Glen Edwards and fumbled. Instead of setting up for a go-ahead touchdown or field goal, the Vikings came away with no points.

Statistics of Super Bowl IX

SCORE BY PERIODS

Pittsburgh Steelers (AFC)	0	2	7	7—16
Minnesota Vikings (NFC)	0	0	0	6— 6

SCORING
Pittsburgh—safety, White downed Tarkenton in end zone
Pittsburgh—Harris 9 run (Gerela kick)

Minnesota—T. Brown recovered blocked punt in end zone (kick failed)

Pittsburgh—L. Brown 4 pass from Bradshaw (Gerela kick)

KEY TEAM STATISTICS

	Pittsburgh	Minnesota
Yards gained rushing	249	17
Yards gained passing	84	102
Total yards gained	333	119
Interceptions thrown	0	3
Fumbles lost	2	2
Total turnovers	2	5
Number of times sacked	2	0
Yardage lost via sacks	12	0

KEY INDIVIDUAL STATISTICS

Pittsburgh

Leading Passer:	Bradshaw	9–14, 96 yards, 1 TD, 0 int.
Leading Rusher:	Harris	34 carries for 158 yards, 1 TD
Leading Receiver:	Brown	3 for 49 yards, 1 TD
Defensive Leader:	Wagner	1 int. (26 yards)
Kicker:	Gerela	2–2 PAT, 0–2 field goals

Minnesota

Leading Passer:	Tarkenton	11–26, 102 yards, 0 TD, 3 int.
Leading Rusher:	Foreman	12 carries for 18 yards
Leading Receiver:	Foreman	5 for 50 yards
Defensive Leaders:	Krause, Poltl	1 fumble recovery each
Kicker:	Cox	0–0 PAT, 0–2 field goals

Super Bowl X—Super Swann

January 18, 1976—Miami, Florida

Pittsburgh wide receiver Lynn Swann almost didn't play in Super Bowl X. He had suffered a concussion during the AFC title game two weeks before, and doctors feared that another blow to the head could be dangerous. But Swann was determined to face the Dallas Cowboys in the big game, and Steelers fans were glad he did.

The Cowboys broke out on top just four minutes into the game, scoring on a 29-yard pass from Roger Staubach to Drew Pearson. Then Pittsburgh quarterback Terry Bradshaw and Swann went to work. Bradshaw told Swann to go long and fast down the sideline. Bradshaw threw the ball in a high arc, sort of like an "alley-oop" pass in basketball. Swann sailed like a bird above Dallas cornerback Mark Washington and came down with the ball on the 7-yard line. Two plays later, the Steelers tied the score, 7–7.

Bradshaw and Swann had still more magic to perform late in the game. With only three minutes remaining, the Steelers were leading 15–10. Bradshaw told Swann to go deep for a bomb again. The Cowboy defense "blitzed" on the play—a fast, surprise rush. Bradshaw waited as long as possible for Swann to get open—almost too long. Dallas defenders crashed into him just as he released the ball. He was knocked to the ground, nearly unconscious, and never saw Swann cross the goal line 64 yards away. The Steelers held Dallas to one touchdown the rest of the way and emerged with a 21–17 victory.

Key play: Along with the two bombs from Bradshaw to Swann, another important play occurred early in the fourth quarter when Pittsburgh's Reggie Harrison blocked a Dallas punt and turned it into a safety. Dallas coach Tom Landry felt that block changed the momentum of the game for the Steelers.

Statistics of Super Bowl X

SCORE BY PERIODS

Pittsburgh Steelers (AFC)	7	0	0	14—	21
Dallas Cowboys (NFC)	7	3	0	7—	17

SCORING

Dallas—D. Pearson 29 pass from Staubach (Fritsch kick)
Pittsburgh—Grossman 7 pass from Bradshaw (Gerela kick)
Dallas—Fritsch field goal (36)
Pittsburgh—safety, Harrison blocked Hoopes's punt in end zone
Pittsburgh—Gerela field goal (36)
Pittsburgh—Gerela field goal (18)
Pittsburgh—Swann 64 pass from Bradshaw (kick failed)
Dallas—F. Howard 34 pass from Staubach (Fritsch kick)

KEY TEAM STATISTICS

	Pittsburgh	Dallas
Yards gained rushing	149	108
Yards gained passing	190	162
Total yards gained	339	270
Interceptions thrown	0	3
Fumbles lost	0	0
Total turnovers	0	3
Number of times sacked	2	7
Yardage lost via sacks	19	42

KEY INDIVIDUAL STATISTICS

Pittsburgh

Leading Passer:	Bradshaw	9–19, 209 yards, 2 TD, 0 int.
Leading Rusher:	Harris	27 carries for 82 yards
Leading Receiver:	Swann	4 for 161 yards, 1 TD
Defensive Leaders:	Edwards, Thomas	1 int. each (both 35 yards)

Kicker:	Gerela	1–2 PAT, 2–4 field goals

Dallas

Leading Passer:	Staubach	15–24, 204 yards, 2 TD, 3 int.
Leading Rusher:	Newhouse	16 carries for 56 yards
Leading Receivers:	D. Pearson	2 for 59 yards, 1 TD
	P. Pearson	5 for 53 yards
Kicker:	Fritsch	2–2 PAT, 1–1 field goals

Super Bowl XI—Raiders Reign

January 9, 1977—Pasadena, California

Super Bowl XI was a matchup of two excellent teams that had gained a reputation for not being able to win the big game. The NFC's Minnesota Vikings were playing in their fourth Super Bowl in eight years but had a record of 0–3 on Super Sunday. Their opponents, the Oakland Raiders, had reached the AFC Championship Game five times in the past six years but had failed each time to win and qualify for the Super Bowl. Vikings coach Bud Grant and Raiders coach John Madden hoped to end their frustrations when their teams squared off before more than 100,000 fans in the Rose Bowl.

The matchup was also one of contrasts. The Vikings were a scrambling team on offense, featuring short passes by Fran Tarkenton and the strong running of Chuck Foreman. The Raiders were known for their wide-open offense, with quarterback Kenny Stabler hurling bombs to wide receivers Fred Biletnikoff and Cliff Branch.

As things turned out, Stabler had a far better day than Tarkenton, Oakland's Clarence Davis gained nearly 100 yards more on the ground than Minny's Foreman, and the Raiders romped to an easy victory, 32–14. Long passes from Stabler to Biletnikoff set up three Raider TDs, and the acrobatic wide receiver was named the game's Most Valuable Player. Oakland also set a record for total offense in the game, 429 yards, that stood for nearly a decade.

Afterwards, Viking coach Grant joked, "We just played them on the wrong day. Next time we'll play them on a Wednesday."

Key play: The Vikings had a chance to get on the scoreboard first following a blocked punt recovered on the Oakland 3-yard line. However, two plays later, Minnesota halfback Brent McClanahan fumbled at the 2-yard line. Oakland got the ball back and started its own successful scoring drive.

Statistics of Super Bowl XI

SCORE BY PERIODS

Oakland Raiders (AFC)	0	16	3	13—32
Minnesota Vikings (NFC)	0	0	7	7—14

SCORING

Oakland—Mann field goal (24)
Oakland—Casper 1 pass from Stabler (Mann kick)
Oakland—Banaszak 1 run (kick failed)
Oakland—Mann field goal (40)
Minnesota—S. White 8 pass from Tarkenton (Cox kick)
Oakland—Banaszak 2 run (Mann kick)
Oakland—Brown 75 interception (kick failed)
Minnesota—Voigt 13 pass from Lee (Cox kick)

KEY TEAM STATISTICS

	Oakland	Minnesota
Yards gained rushing	266	71
Yards gained passing	163	282
Total yards gained	429	353

Interceptions thrown	0	2
Fumbles lost	0	1
Total turnovers	0	3
Number of times sacked	2	1
Yardage lost via sacks	17	4

KEY INDIVIDUAL STATISTICS
Oakland

Leading Passer:	Stabler	12–19, 180 yards, 1 TD, 0 int.
Leading Rushers:	Davis	16 carries for 137 yards
	Banaszak	10 carries for 19 yards, 2 TD
Leading Receivers:	Biletnikoff	4 for 79 yards
	Casper	4 for 70 yards, 1 TD
Defensive Leader:	Brown	1 int. (75 yards, TD)
Kicker:	Mann	2–4 PAT, 2–3 field goals

Minnesota

Leading Passers:	Tarkenton	17–35, 205 yards, 1 TD, 2 int.
	Lee	7–9, 81 yards, 1 TD, 0 int.
Leading Rusher:	Foreman	17 carries for 44 yards
Leading Receiver:	S. White	5 for 77 yards, 1 TD
Kicker:	Cox	2–2 PAT, 0–0 field goals

Super Bowl XII—Dallas Derails Denver
January 15, 1978—New Orleans, Louisiana

Before Super Bowl XII began, the two opposing quarter-backs—Roger Staubach of the Dallas Cowboys and Craig Morton of the Denver Broncos—met at midfield and hugged. They were old friends from the days they had both played for Dallas. Morton had led the Cowboys in Super Bowl V, and Staubach had been the team's quarterback in

Super Bowl VI. Then the two men separated and went to different sides of the field to begin their battle.

It was no contest, really. Staubach directed the Cowboys on scoring drives in each period to key an easy 27–10 win. The Cowboys' offensive attack was balanced between passes and runs. Staubach alternated throws to receivers Preston Pearson, Billy Joe DuPree, and Butch Johnson with handoffs to running backs Tony Dorsett and Robert Newhouse.

But the real heroes of the day for Dallas were the team's defensive linemen. Two big rushers, Harvey Martin and Randy White, were named co-MVPs of the contest. Under intense pressure from the Cowboy defensive line all day, Morton completed as many passes to the defenders as he did to his teammates. He threw four completions and four interceptions. Denver coach Red Miller mercifully removed Morton from the game in the third period and replaced him with backup Norris Weese. Weese directed the team's only touchdown drive.

Key play: The game featured one spectacular play by the Cowboys. Midway through the fourth quarter, Staubach pitched the ball to halfback Robert Newhouse on a sweep to the right. Newhouse stopped quickly and arched a pass downfield. Dallas receiver Golden Richards made a great over-the-head catch for the Cowboys' final score.

Statistics of Super Bowl XII

SCORE BY PERIODS

Denver Broncos (AFC)	0	0	10	0—10
Dallas Cowboys (NFC)	10	3	7	7—27

SCORING
Dallas—Dorsett 3 run (Herrera kick)

Dallas—Herrera field goal (35)
Dallas—Herrera field goal (43)
Denver—Turner field goal (47)
Dallas—Johnson 45 pass from Staubach (Herrera kick)
Denver—Lytle 1 run (Turner kick)
Dallas—Richards 29 pass from Newhouse (Herrera kick)

KEY TEAM STATISTICS

	Denver	Dallas
Yards gained rushing	121	143
Yards gained passing	35	182
Total yards gained	156	325
Interceptions thrown	4	0
Fumbles lost	4	2
Total turnovers	8	2
Number of times sacked	4	5
Yardage lost via sacks	26	35

KEY INDIVIDUAL STATISTICS

Denver

Leading Passer:	Morton	4–15, 39 yards, 0 TD, 4 int.
Leading Rusher:	Lytle	10 carries for 35 yards, 1 TD
Leading Receiver:	Dolbin	2 for 24
Kicker:	Turner	1–1 PAT, 1–1 field goals

Dallas

Leading Passer:	Staubach	17–25, 183 yards, 1 TD, 0 int.
Leading Rusher:	Dorsett	15 carries for 66 yards, 1 TD
Leading Receiver:	P. Pearson	5 for 37 yards
Defensive Leader:	Kyle	1 int., 1 fumble recovery
Kicker:	Herrera	3–3 PAT, 2–5 field goals

Super Bowl XIII—Terry is Tops

January 21, 1979—Miami, Florida

Super Bowl XIII marked the first time the same two teams had faced off again on a Super Sunday. The Pittsburgh Steelers and Dallas Cowboys had met three years before in Super Bowl X, with Pittsburgh edging out Dallas, 21–17. The final score of Super Bowl XIII turned out to be just as close, but the game was even wilder.

The contest had a little bit of everything in it. First, the Cowboys tried a trick double-reverse play that might have led to a score, but Drew Pearson fumbled the ball to end the threat. Seven plays later, Pittsburgh quarterback Terry Bradshaw hit John Stallworth with a beautiful 28-yard pass to put the Steelers up 7–0. Dallas came right back with two touchdowns, one on a fumble recovery and runback by linebacker Mike Hegman. Then Pittsburgh rebounded with a short Bradshaw pass that Stallworth turned into a long 75-yard TD. At halftime Pittsburgh was up 21–14, and Terry Bradshaw was having an outstanding day.

In the third period, Dallas was on the Pittsburgh 10-yard line, ready to score the tying touchdown. Tight end Jackie Smith was all alone in the end zone. Unbelievably, Smith, a future Hall of Famer, dropped the ball. After the play was over, he lay broken-hearted for several seconds on the ground. Later he told reporters, "I just missed it. I slipped a little, but I still should have caught it. I've dropped passes before, but never any that was so important."

The Cowboys kicked a field goal on the next play but still trailed in the game and never caught up again. Bradshaw engineered two more Pittsburgh scoring drives, and the Steelers held on as Dallas frantically scored 14 points in the last three minutes of the game. When the gun sounded to end the contest, Pittsburgh was ahead 35–31 in the second-highest scoring game in Super

44

Bowl history. The Steelers made history also by becoming the first three-time Super Bowl winner. And Bradshaw, the game's MVP, proved he was one of the best quarterbacks ever to play in the NFL.

Key play: One of the biggest plays of the game occurred in the fourth quarter with Pittsburgh ahead 28–17. Roy Gerela's squibbed kickoff was picked up by Dallas lineman Randy White. White, who was playing with a broken arm, fumbled the ball, and the Steelers recovered. Bradshaw hit Lynn Swann with an 18-yard touchdown pass on the next play.

Statistics of Super Bowl XIII

SCORE BY PERIODS

Pittsburgh Steelers (AFC)	7	14	0	14—35
Dallas Cowboys (NFC)	7	7	3	14—31

SCORING

Pittsburgh—Stallworth 28 pass from Bradshaw (Gerela kick)

Dallas—Hill 39 pass from Staubach (Septien kick)

Dallas—Hegman 37 fumble recovery (Septien kick)

Pittsburgh—Stallworth 75 pass from Bradshaw (Gerela kick)

Pittsburgh—Bleier 7 pass from Bradshaw (Gerela kick)

Dallas—Septien field goal (27)

Pittsburgh—Harris 22 run (Gerela kick)

Pittsburgh—Swann 18 pass from Bradshaw (Gerela kick)

Dallas—DuPree 7 pass from Staubach (Septien kick)

Dallas—B. Johnson 4 pass from Staubach (Septien kick)

KEY TEAM STATISTICS

	Pittsburgh	Dallas
Yards gained rushing	66	154
Yards gained passing	291	176
Total yards gained	357	330
Interceptions thrown	1	1
Fumbles lost	2	2
Total turnovers	3	3
Number of times sacked	4	5
Yardage lost via sacks	27	52

KEY INDIVIDUAL STATISTICS
Pittsburgh

Leading Passer:	Bradshaw	17–30, 318 yards, 4 TD, 1 int.
Leading Rusher:	Harris	20 carries for 68 yards, 1 TD
Leading Receivers:	Swann	7 for 124 yards, 1 TD
	Stallworth	3 for 115 yards, 2 TD
Defensive Leader:	Blount	1 int. (13 yards)
Kicker:	Gerela	5–5 PAT, 0–1 field goals

Dallas

Leading Passer:	Staubach	17–30, 228 yards, 3 TD, 1 int.
Leading Rusher:	Dorsett	16 carries for 96 yards
Leading Receivers:	D. Pearson	4 for 73 yards
	Dorsett	5 for 44 yards
Kicker:	Septien	4–4 PAT, 1–1 field goals

Super Bowl XIV—Steelers Rip the Rams
January 20, 1980—Pasadena, California

The Pittsburgh Steelers had won three Super Bowls in the 1970s and hoped to start the new decade with a fourth NFL title. Most of the same cast was in place: Bradshaw,

Harris, Bleier, Swann, Stallworth, Lambert, Greene, and Blount.

The team across the field—the Los Angeles Rams—had never been in a Super Bowl before. In fact, many fans were surprised they had won the 1979 NFC championship after compiling a mediocre 9–7 regular season record. But the Rams had beaten Dallas and Tampa Bay in the playoffs and had earned the right to meet Pittsburgh in the Rose Bowl.

The Rams quickly proved they were not intimidated by the Steelers. After Pittsburgh scored a field goal on its first possession of the game, Los Angeles came right back with a touchdown to go ahead, 7–3. The Rams, amazingly, were still ahead after three quarters, 19–17.

The Steelers' All-Star middle linebacker Jack Lambert was particularly concerned that his club seemed to be asleep on both offense and defense. Lambert came into the Pittsburgh huddle one time and let out an earsplitting roar. "He bellowed so loud that I kind of got scared," a teammate said. The roar woke the Steelers up, and they went on to score 14 fourth-quarter points to ice the win.

Key play: Lambert also made a critical interception in the fourth quarter to stop a Los Angeles drive that might have put the Rams ahead near the end of the game.

Statistics of Super Bowl XIV

SCORE BY PERIODS

Pittsburgh Steelers (AFC)	3	7	7	14—31
Los Angeles Rams (NFC)	7	6	6	0—19

SCORING
Pittsburgh—Bahr field goal (41)
Los Angeles—Bryant 1 run (Corral kick)

Pittsburgh—Harris 1 run (Bahr kick)

Los Angeles—Corral field goal (31)

Los Angeles—Corral field goal (45)

Pittsburgh—Swann 47 pass from Bradshaw (Bahr kick)

Los Angeles—Smith 24 pass from McCutcheon (kick failed)

Pittsburgh—Stallworth 73 pass from Bradshaw (Bahr kick)

Pittsburgh—Harris 1 run (Bahr kick)

KEY TEAM STATISTICS

	Pittsburgh	Los Angeles
Yards gained rushing	84	107
Yards gained passing	309	194
Total yards gained	393	301
Interceptions thrown	3	1
Fumbles lost	0	0
Total turnovers	3	1
Number of times sacked	0	4
Yardage lost via sacks	0	42

KEY INDIVIDUAL STATISTICS
Pittsburgh

Leading Passer:	Bradshaw	14–21, 309 yards, 2 TD, 3 int.
Leading Rusher:	Harris	20 carries for 46 yards, 2 TD
Leading Receivers:	Swann	5 for 79 yards, 1 TD
	Stallworth	3 for 121 yards, 1 TD
Defensive Leader:	Lambert	1 int. (16 yards)
Kicker:	Bahr	4–4 PAT, 1–1 field goals

Los Angeles

Leading Passer:	Ferragamo	15–25, 212 yards, 0 TD, 1 int.

Leading Rusher:	Tyler	17 carries for 60 yards
Leading Receivers:	Bryant	3 for 21 yards
	Waddy	3 for 75 yards
Kicker:	Corral	1–2 PAT, 2–2 field goals

Super Bowl XV—Plunkett Proves Himself
January 25, 1981—New Orleans, Louisiana

When the Oakland Raiders made it to Super Bowl XV, most people were surprised. Sportswriters had predicted that the club would finish last in its division in the AFC. Instead, the Raiders had come in second. They had made the playoffs as a "wild card," an extra team added to the playoffs along with the division winners.

The biggest question mark about the Raiders was their quarterback, Jim Plunkett. Plunkett had been terrific in the early 1970s with the New England Patriots, but bad knees and a sore arm had almost forced him to quit football in 1978. Raiders coach Tom Flores convinced him not to retire, and he repaid the coach with several outstanding years in Oakland.

Outstanding was a good word to describe Plunkett's performance in Super Bowl XV against the Philadelphia Eagles. In the first quarter, Oakland was on the Eagles' 2-yard line. Plunkett called a pass play, but no receivers were open. He scrambled around in the backfield, bad knees and all, until Cliff Branch got open, and then zipped the ball to Branch for the game's first score. A few moments later, Plunkett hurled a bomb to running back Kenny King for a Super Bowl record 80-yard touchdown. That gave the Raiders a commanding 14–0 lead before the first quarter was over. In the third period, Plunkett found Branch again for a 29-yard TD that put the game out of reach of the Eagles. The final score was Oakland 27, Philadelphia 10.

Key play: Rod Martin set the tone for the day when he intercepted Eagles quarterback Ron Jaworski's first pass of the afternoon and ran it back deep into Philadelphia territory. A few plays later, Plunkett found Branch in the end zone to put Oakland ahead for good. Martin would earn a place in the Super Bowl record book that day by intercepting three passes thrown by Jaworski.

Statistics of Super Bowl XV

SCORE BY PERIODS

Oakland Raiders (AFC)	14	0	10	3—27
Philadelphia Eagles (NFC)	0	3	0	7—10

SCORING
Oakland—Branch 2 pass from Plunkett (Bahr kick)
Oakland—King 80 pass from Plunkett (Bahr kick)
Philadelphia—Franklin field goal (30)
Oakland—Branch 29 pass from Plunkett (Bahr kick)
Oakland—Bahr field goal (46)
Philadelphia—Krepfle 8 pass from Jaworski (Franklin kick)
Oakland—Bahr field goal (35)

KEY TEAM STATISTICS

	Oakland	Philadelphia
Yards gained rushing	117	69
Yards gained passing	260	291
Total yards gained	377	360
Interceptions thrown	0	3
Fumbles lost	0	1
Total turnovers	0	4
Number of times sacked	1	0
Yardage lost via sacks	1	0

Oakland

Leading Passer:	Plunkett	13–21, 261 yards, 3 TD, 0 int.
Leading Rusher:	van Eeghen	19 carries for 80 yards
Leading Receiver:	Branch	5 for 67 yards, 2 TD
Defensive Leader:	Martin	3 int. (44 yards)
Kicker:	Bahr	3–3 PAT, 2–3 field goals

Philadelphia

Leading Passer:	Jaworski	18–38, 291 yards, 1 TD, 3 int.
Leading Rusher:	Montgomery	16 carries for 44 yards
Leading Receivers:	Montgomery	6 for 91 yards
	Carmichael	5 for 83 yards
Kicker:	Franklin	1–1 PAT, 1–2 field goals

Super Bowl XVI—Montana's Magic

January 24, 1982—Pontiac, Michigan

Super Bowl XVI featured several "firsts." For the first time ever, a northern city was hosting the NFL championship game. The contest was held inside the Pontiac Silverdome near Detroit. Outside the windchill was below zero, but inside the temperature was a comfortable 72 degrees. The two opposing teams were also making their first-ever appearances in a Super Bowl. The San Francisco 49ers had been in the NFL since 1946 but had never before played for a league championship. The Cincinnati Bengals had made the playoffs only twice in their 14-year history and had never won a title.

Both Super Bowl opponents had another important connection. Bill Walsh, head coach of the 49ers, had once been the quarterback coach of the Bengals. Walsh had trained both San Francisco's Joe Montana and Cincinnati's Ken Anderson to become two of the top passers in pro football.

51

On this day, Anderson would record the better overall statistics, but Montana would make the bigger plays and earn his first Super Bowl ring.

Montana's best quality was his determination. He never gave up. To get the 49ers into the Super Bowl, Montana had directed the club on an 89-yard drive to overtake the Dallas Cowboys, 28–27, in the final minute of the NFC championship game.

In the Super Bowl Montana began weaving his magic early. He directed the 49ers on two typical long, slow drives for first-half touchdowns. Placekicker Ray Wersching added two field goals to put the Niners up 20–0 at the half. To get the Bengals back in the game in the second half, Anderson threw pass after pass to tight end Dan Ross and wide receiver Chris Collinsworth. He even ran for Cincinnati's first touchdown with a scramble up the middle. The Bengals got as close as 20–14 early in the fourth period. However, two more Wersching field goals helped San Francisco hold on for a 26–21 win.

Key play: There were really four key plays in a row in the game. In the third period, Cincinnati had a first down on the 49ers 3-yard line. Four times the Bengals tried to pound the ball across the goal line, and four times San Francisco's defense turned them away. A touchdown might have turned the tide for Cincinnati.

Statistics of Super Bowl XVI

SCORE BY PERIODS
Cincinnati Bengals (AFC)	0	0	7	14—21
San Francisco 49ers (NFC)	7	13	0	6—26

SCORING
San Francisco—Montana 1 run (Wersching kick)

San Francisco—Cooper 11 pass from Montana (Wersching kick)
San Francisco—Wersching field goal (22)
San Francisco—Wersching field goal (26)
Cincinnati—Anderson 5 run (Breech kick)
Cincinnati—Ross 4 pass from Anderson (Breech kick)
San Francisco—Wersching field goal (40)
San Francisco—Wersching field goal (23)
Cincinnati—Ross 3 pass from Anderson (Breech kick)

KEY TEAM STATISTICS

	Cincinnati	San Francisco
Yards gained rushing	72	127
Yards gained passing	284	148
Total yards gained	356	275
Interceptions thrown	2	0
Fumbles lost	2	1
Total turnovers	4	1
Number of times sacked	5	1
Yardage lost via sacks	16	9

KEY INDIVIDUAL STATISTICS
Cincinnati
Leading Passer:	Anderson	25–34, 300 yards, 2 TD, 2 int.
Leading Rusher:	Johnson	14 carries for 36 yards
Leading Receiver:	Ross	11 for 104 yards, 2 TD
Kicker:	Breech	3–3 PAT, 0–0 field goals

San Francisco
Leading Passer:	Montana	14–22, 157 yards, 1 TD, 0 int.
Leading Rusher:	Patton	17 carries for 55 yards
Leading Receivers:	Solomon	4 for 52 yards
	Clark	4 for 45 yards

Defensive Leaders:	Hicks,	
	Wright	1 int. each
Kicker:	Wersching	2–2 PAT, 4–4 field goals

Super Bowl XVII—Riggins and the Redskins
January 30, 1983—Pasadena, California

It had been ten years since the Washington Redskins and Miami Dolphins had met in a Super Bowl. But Washington fans still remembered their club's 14–7 loss to the undefeated Dolphins in Super Bowl VII. They were eager for revenge.

Super Bowl XVII was a classic matchup. The Redskins had a powerful offense, with 230-pound halfback John Riggins and quarterback Joe Theismann leading the way. The Dolphins were famous for their defensive unit, which was called the "Killer Bees" because the last names of six starting defenders began with the letter *B*.

Football experts predicted a close game, and they were right. With ten minutes to go, Miami was up, 17–13. The Redskins had the ball on fourth down on the Dolphin 43-yard line. Everyone on the field, in the stands, and watching on television knew Riggins was going to get the ball to try for a first down. Could the Dolphins stop him?

As the play began, a Miami defender slipped and fell. Riggins took the handoff and went right for that spot. The defender tried to stop Riggins with one arm, but that was like trying to halt a locomotive with a flyswatter. Riggins broke the tackle and several others, outracing the entire Miami defensive unit to the goal line. That play broke open the game. Washington went on to win its first Super Bowl, 27–17, and Riggins was named Most Valuable Player.

Key play: Late in the third period, Miami's Kim Bokamper tipped a Joe Theismann pass into the air and waited for it to come down. He was going to catch it and score an easy touchdown. Instead, Theismann jumped up and knocked the ball to the ground for a harmless incompletion.

Statistics of Super Bowl XVII

SCORE BY PERIODS

Miami Dolphins (AFC)	7	10	0	0—17
Washington Redskins (NFC)	0	10	3	14—27

SCORING

Miami—Cefalo 76 pass from Woodley (von Schamann kick)

Washington—Moseley field goal (31)

Miami—von Schamann field goal (20)

Washington—Garrett 4 pass from Theismann (Moseley kick)

Miami—Walker 98 kickoff return (von Schamann kick)

Washington—Moseley field goal (20)

Washington—Riggins 43 run (Moseley kick)

Washington—Brown 6 pass from Theismann (Moseley kick)

KEY TEAM STATISTICS

	Miami	Washington
Yards gained rushing	96	276
Yards gained passing	80	124
Total yards gained	176	400
Interceptions thrown	1	2
Fumbles lost	1	0
Total turnovers	2	2
Number of times sacked	1	3
Yardage lost via sacks	17	19

KEY INDIVIDUAL STATISTICS
Miami

Leading Passer:	Woodley	4–14, 97 yards, 1 TD, 1 int.
Leading Rusher:	Franklin	16 carries for 49 yards
Leading Receiver:	Cefalo	2 for 82 yards, 1 TD
Kicker:	von Schamann	2–2 PAT, 1–1 field goals

Washington

Leading Passer:	Theismann	15–23, 143 yards, 2 TD, 2 int.
Leading Rusher:	Riggins	38 carries for 166 yards, 1 TD
Leading Receiver:	Brown	5 for 60 yards, 1 TD
Kicker:	Moseley	3–3 PAT, 2–2 field goals

Super Bowl XVIII— Raiders Wreck the Redskins

January 22, 1984—Tampa, Florida

The rushing record that John Riggins set in Super Bowl XVII lasted just one year. In Super Bowl XVIII, Marcus Allen of the Los Angeles (formerly Oakland) Raiders easily surpassed Riggins's mark. Allen totaled 191 yards on 20 carries and also scored two touchdowns. Just as easily, the Raiders crushed the favored Redskins in a shocking 38–9 rout.

Los Angeles scored on offense and on defense during the first half. L.A. quarterback Jim Plunkett, the hero of Super Bowl XV, passed for one touchdown, and Raider defenders blocked a Washington punt into the end zone and returned a pass interception for two more scores.

In the third quarter, Allen took over. He burst through a hole in the Washington line for a 5-yard touchdown early in the period. Later, he turned a broken play into a spectacular run. Allen took the ball from Plunkett and headed toward his left. When he spotted a group of Redskins tacklers there, he simply changed direction and broke away to the right and ran for a record 74-yard score. One of Allen's blockers said it looked like "a rocket" was going by on that play. Allen was a clear choice as the game's Most Valuable Player.

Key play: With 12 seconds left in the first half, Washington quarterback Joe Theismann tried to trick the Raiders with a screen pass from his own 12-yard line. Theismann was the one who was surprised, however, when Los Angeles linebacker Jack Squirek picked off the soft pass and raced into the end zone for a Raiders touchdown and a 21–3 lead.

Statistics of Super Bowl XVIII

SCORE BY PERIODS

Los Angeles Raiders (AFC)	7	14	14	3—38
Washington Redskins (NFC)	0	3	6	0— 9

SCORING

Los Angeles—Jensen recovered blocked punt in end zone (Bahr kick)

Los Angeles—Branch 12 pass from Plunkett (Bahr kick)

Washington—Moseley field goal (24)

Los Angeles—Squirek 5 interception return (Bahr kick)

Washington—Riggins 1 run (kick blocked)

Los Angeles—Allen 5 run (Bahr kick)

Los Angeles—Allen 74 run (Bahr kick)

Los Angeles—Bahr field goal (21)

KEY TEAM STATISTICS

	Los Angeles	Washington
Yards gained rushing	231	90
Yards gained passing	154	193
Total yards gained	385	283
Interceptions thrown	0	2
Fumbles lost	2	1
Total turnovers	2	3
Number of times sacked	2	6
Yardage lost via sacks	18	50

KEY INDIVIDUAL STATISTICS
Los Angeles

Leading Passer:	Plunkett	16–25, 172 yards, 1 TD, 0 int.
Leading Rusher:	Allen	20 carries for 191 yards, 2 TD
Leading Receiver:	Branch	6 for 94 yards, 1 TD
Defensive Leader:	Squirek	1 int. (5 yards, TD)
Kicker:	Bahr	5–5 PAT, 1–1 field goals

Washington

Leading Passer:	Theismann	16–35, 243 yards, 0 TD, 2 int.
Leading Rusher:	Riggins	26 carries for 64 yards, 1 TD
Leading Receiver:	Didier	5 for 65 yards
Kicker:	Moseley	0–1 PAT, 1–2 field goals

Super Bowl XIX—Montana Meets Marino
January 20, 1985—Palo Alto, California

Everyone knew what to expect when the San Francisco 49ers and Miami Dolphins squared off in Super Bowl XIX. The two clubs featured the most exciting quarterbacks in the NFL, San Francisco's Joe Montana and Miami's Dan Marino. This game was bound to be a wide-open, high-scoring affair. And it was! Super Bowl XIX is the only one in which both quarterbacks threw for more than 300 yards.

Marino struck first, completing his first pass of the day to running back Tony Nathan for 25 yards. A few minutes later, Miami kicker Uwe von Schamann connected on a 37-yard field goal for a 3–0 Dolphin lead. Marino had made it look easy.

Montana led the 49ers right back, hitting halfback Carl Monroe for a 33-yard score to put San Francisco ahead, 7–3. Then Marino pushed the Dolphins the other way down the field for a go-ahead touchdown. Turning their heads from side to side, fans probably began to think they were watching a tennis match.

Unfortunately for Dolphins fans, Miami proved no match for San Francisco this day. Marino's passing arm was just not strong enough to balance the Niners' offensive combination. The 49ers not only had Montana's passing and scrambling ability, they also featured the running of halfbacks Wendell Tyler and Roger Craig. The three stars helped San Francisco set a record with over 500 total yards during the game. The Dolphins, meanwhile, could generate only 25 yards rushing to go along with Marino's passing and fell easily, 38–16.

Key play: Early in the second period, Miami defenders thought they had Montana trapped behind the line of scrimmage, but he scrambled around them. He gained 19 yards and a first down. A few plays later, the 49ers went ahead for good, 14–10.

Statistics of Super Bowl XIX

SCORE BY PERIODS

Miami Dolphins (AFC)	10	6	0	0—16
San Francisco 49ers (NFC)	7	21	10	0—38

SCORING

Miami—von Schamann field goal (37)

San Francisco—Monroe 33 pass from Montana (Wersching kick)

Miami—D. Johnson 2 pass from Marino (van Schamann kick)

San Francisco—Montana 6 run (Wersching kick)

San Francisco—Craig 2 run (Wersching kick)

Miami—von Schamann field goal (31)

Miami—von Schamann field goal (30)

San Francisco—Wersching field goal (27)

San Francisco—Craig 16 pass from Montana (Wersching kick)

KEY TEAM STATISTICS

	Miami	San Francisco
Yards gained rushing	25	211
Yards gained passing	289	326
Total yards gained	314	537
Interceptions thrown	2	0
Fumbles lost	0	2
Total turnovers	2	2
Number of times sacked	4	1
Yardage lost via sacks	29	5

KEY INDIVIDUAL STATISTICS
Miami

Leading Passer:	Marino	29–50, 318 yards, 1 TD, 2 int.

Leading Rusher:	Nathan	5 carries for 18 yards
Leading Receivers:	Nathan	10 for 83 yards
	Clayton	6 for 92 yards
Kicker:	von Schamann	1–1 PAT, 3–3 field goals

San Francisco

Leading Passer:	Montana	24–35, 331 yards, 3 TD, 0 int.
Leading Rushers:	Tyler	13 carries for 65 yards
	Craig	15 carries for 58 yards, 1 TD
	Montana	5 carries for 59 yards, 1 TD
Leading Receivers:	Craig	7 for 77 yards, 2 TD
	Clark	6 for 77 yards
Kicker:	Wersching	5–5 PAT, 1–1 field goals

Super Bowl XX—A Powerful Bear Hug

January 26, 1986—New Orleans, Louisiana

The Super Bowl was celebrating its 20th birthday. It was fitting that one of the guests was the NFL's oldest team, the Chicago Bears. The Bears had won the first NFL championship game in 1933. Now they were heavy favorites to whip the New England Patriots and earn their first Super Bowl victory.

The Bears had compiled an awesome 17–1 record coming into Super Bowl XX. They were a mixture of heroes and weirdos. Chicago running back Walter Payton was the NFL's all-time leading ground gainer. Football fans had been hoping for years that he would get a chance to show off his talent in a Super Bowl. The Bears' defense was led by linebacker Mike Singletary and end Richard Dent, two very intense players. They took great pride in shutting down the opposition.

Chicago's defense had not allowed a single point so far in the playoffs.

On the strange side, there were Chicago quarterback Jim McMahon and defensive lineman and occasional fullback William "the Refrigerator" Perry. McMahon was a free spirit who usually did things his own way. Perry weighed well over 300 pounds and earned his nickname because he was built like a huge kitchen refrigerator. He was not only good at stopping other teams' runners, but he was sometimes called on to carry the ball himself on plays near the goal line. Perry would use his bulk to push through defenders and score.

Across the field were the New England Patriots. No one had expected them to reach the Super Bowl, but they loved being underdogs. As a "wild card" team, they had been forced to win three playoff games on the road to become AFC champs. New England's strengths were its running game, keyed by backs Craig James and Tony Collins, and a powerful offensive line.

Most football fans thought the Bears would crush New England easily. But Pats fans hoped this Super Bowl would have the same ending as the David and Goliath story in the Bible, with underdog David defeating the powerful giant. The game seemed to start off that way. On the second play of the contest, Walter Payton fumbled and New England's Larry McGrew recovered on the Bears 19-yard line. Three plays later, Tony Franklin kicked a 36-yard field goal to give the Pats a 3–0 lead with only 1:19 gone off the clock. It was the fastest score in Super Bowl history.

It was also the last time that New England would get on the scoreboard until late in the game. Meanwhile, the Bears made five touchdowns and three field goals on their way to a 46–10 victory. That was the most lopsided score yet in a Super Bowl.

The Bears were simply awesome. Richard Dent was

named the game's Most Valuable Player, but the whole defensive unit deserved the award. They held New England's powerful runners to just seven yards on the ground. McMahon scored twice on short runs and had a great day passing. Even "the Refrigerator" chilled out by rushing for a touchdown.

Key play: Early in the third quarter, the Pats had Chicago backed up on its 4-yard line. McMahon told receiver Willie Gault to go long. Then he faded back into the end zone and hurled a 60-yard bomb to Gault to get the Bears out of trouble.

Statistics of Super Bowl XX

SCORE BY PERIODS

New England Patriots (AFC)	3	0	0	7—10
Chicago Bears (NFC)	13	10	21	2—46

SCORING
New England—Franklin field goal (36)
Chicago—Butler field goal (28)
Chicago—Butler field goal (24)
Chicago—Suhey 11 run (Butler kick)
Chicago—McMahon 2 run (Butler kick)
Chicago—Butler field goal (24)
Chicago—McMahon 1 run (Butler kick)
Chicago—Phillips 28 interception return (Butler kick)
Chicago—Perry 1 run (Butler kick)
New England—Fryar 8 pass from Grogan (Franklin kick)
Chicago—safety, Grogan tackled by Waechter in end zone

KEY TEAM STATISTICS

	New England	Chicago
Yards gained rushing	7	167
Yards gained passing	116	241

Total yards gained	123	408
Interceptions thrown	2	0
Fumbles lost	4	2
Total turnovers	6	2
Number of times sacked	7	3
Yardage lost via sacks	61	15

KEY INDIVIDUAL STATISTICS
New England
Leading Passer:	Grogan	17–30, 177 yards, 1 TD, 2 int.
Leading Rusher:	Collins	3 carries for 4 yards
Leading Receiver:	Morgan	7 for 70 yards
Kicker:	Franklin	1–1 PAT, 1–1 field goals

Chicago
Leading Passer:	McMahon	12–20, 256 yards, 0 TD, 0 int.
Leading Rushers:	Payton	22 carries for 61 yards
	Suhey	11 carries for 52 yards, 1 TD
	McMahon	5 carries for 14 yards, 2 TD
Leading Receiver:	Gault	4 for 129 yards
Defensive Leaders:	Singletary	2 fumble recoveries
	Phillips	1 int. (28 yards, TD)
Kicker:	Butler	5–5 PAT, 3–3 field goals

Super Bowl XXI—The Giants Stand Tall
January 25, 1987—Pasadena, California

Longtime professional football fans had been thrilled when the Chicago Bears won Super Bowl XX. They were just as excited to see the New York Giants earn a Super Bowl berth following the 1986 season. Like the Bears, the Giants had a long and glorious history in the National

Football League. And, like the Bears, the Giants had spent many years struggling to return to their former glory. New York's fortunes began to improve when the club made a little-known college quarterback named Phil Simms its top draft pick in 1979. Simms had a rough time his first few years in New York and was often sidelined with injuries. In 1983 he was demoted to second-string quarterback and asked to be traded. Luckily, the Giants didn't grant his wish.

The next year Bill Parcells took over as Giants head coach. Building around All-Stars Lawrence Taylor and Harry Carson, Parcells fashioned one of the most dangerous defensive units in the league. And building around Simms, running back Joe Morris, and tight end Mark Bavaro, Parcells constructed a solid offensive attack. The well-balanced Giants roared into the Super Bowl following playoff routs of 49–3 over San Francisco and 17–0 over Washington.

The Giants were not the only team excited to be playing in Super Bowl XXI. Across the field, the Denver Broncos paced the sidelines waiting for the opening kickoff. The Broncos felt lucky to be playing for the NFL championship. Just two weeks before, in the AFC title game against Cleveland, the Broncos were trailing 20–13 with time running out. Denver's All-Pro quarterback John Elway then directed a masterful 98-yard drive to tie the score with seconds remaining. The big quarterback took charge in overtime, too, setting up a winning field goal. Elway hoped he would have the same success in the Super Bowl.

Super Bowl XXI turned out to be two games in one. The first half was a tight struggle. The second half was a blowout.

Denver scored first in the game on a Rich Karlis field goal. Then New York took the lead on a drive in which Simms completed all six of his passes. The last completion went to Zeke Mowatt for a touchdown. It was Elway's turn next. He passed the Broncos to the Giants'

4-yard line and then ran the ball in himself to put Denver back ahead, 10–7.

After Denver's defense held New York, Elway engineered another drive that could have put Denver in control of the game. However, the famous Giants defense made a great goal-line stand to keep Denver from scoring. At halftime the Broncos were still on top, 10–9.

The second half was an entirely different contest. Simms came out of the locker room on fire. He completed nearly every pass he threw as the Giants scored four touchdowns and a field goal to blow Denver out of the game. By the end, New York was a 39–20 winner, and Simms was the MVP. He had completed a remarkable 22 of 25 passes. The next day, headlines around the country read: "Phil is Simmsational."

Key play: The Giants' defense was fired up after their goal-line stand. The next time Denver got the ball, defensive end George Martin broke through the Bronco line and sacked Elway for a 13-yard loss and safety. That play made New York feel "unbeatable."

Statistics of Super Bowl XXI

SCORE BY PERIODS

Denver Broncos (AFC)	10	0	0	10—20
New York Giants (NFC)	7	2	17	13—39

SCORING

Denver—Karlis field goal (48)
New York—Mowatt 6 pass from Simms (Allegre kick)
Denver—Elway 4 run (Karlis kick)
New York—safety, Elway sacked by Martin in end zone
New York—Bavaro 13 pass from Simms (Allegre kick)
New York—Allegre field goal (21)

New York—Morris 1 run (Allegre kick)
New York—McConkey 6 pass from Simms (Allegre kick)
Denver—Karlis field goal (28)
New York—Anderson 2 run (kick failed)
Denver—V. Johnson 47 pass from Elway (Karlis kick)

<u>KEY TEAM STATISTICS</u>

	Denver	New York
Yards gained rushing	52	136
Yards gained passing	320	263
Total yards gained	372	399
Interceptions thrown	1	0
Fumbles lost	0	0
Total turnovers	1	0
Number of times sacked	4	1
Yardage lost via sacks	32	5

<u>KEY INDIVIDUAL STATISTICS</u>
Denver

Leading Passer:	Elway	22–37, 304 yards, 1 TD, 1 int.
Leading Rusher:	Elway	6 carries for 27 yards, 1 TD
Leading Receiver:	V. Johnson	5 for 121 yards, 1 TD
Kicker:	Karlis	2–2 PAT, 2–4 field goals

New York

Leading Passer:	Simms	22–25, 268 yards, 3 TD, 0 int.
Leading Rusher:	Morris	20 carries for 67 yards, 1 TD
Leading Receiver:	Bavaro	4 for 51, 1 TD
Defensive Leader:	Martin	sacked Elway for safety
Kicker:	Allegre	4–5 PAT, 1–1 field goals

Super Bowl XXII—Williams the Conqueror

January 31, 1988—San Diego, California

The Denver Broncos, smarting from their defeat the previous year, were back for another try to capture the NFL championship in Super Bowl XXII. Their opponents were the Washington Redskins. Both clubs had added incentive for winning the big game. Neither wanted to become the first club besides the Minnesota Vikings to lose three Super Bowls.

While the Broncos were pretty much the same team as had played the year before, the Redskins were a very different squad from the one that had won Super Bowl XVII and lost Super Bowl XVIII. Both Joe Theismann and John Riggins were gone. Their replacements were Doug Williams at quarterback and Timmy Smith at running back. Neither man had been a starter for the Redskins when the season began, but both had worked their way into the lineup. Many experts didn't have high opinions of either Williams or Smith before Super Bowl XXII. However, they certainly changed their minds afterwards.

Because of Denver's experience and the presence of John Elway at quarterback, the Broncos were favorites to win. And they looked like winners in the early going. Denver scored on its first two possessions and raced out to a 10–0 first quarter lead on an Elway TD pass and a Rich Karlis field goal.

As if things weren't going badly enough for Washington, Williams injured his ankle near the end of the first period and had to be carried off the field. Trainers taped Williams's ankle tightly, and a few minutes later he limped back onto the field.

No one could have predicted what would happen next. Early in the second quarter, Williams called for a short pass to wide receiver Ricky Sanders. But Sanders was covered tightly by his defender at the line of scrimmage, so he decided to go long. Williams sent a beautiful spiral downfield that Sanders caught on the full run and turned into an 80-yard touchdown. That play tied the record for the longest pass completion in Super Bowl history.

Williams wasn't through, however. Over the next 12 minutes, he completed three more touchdown strikes and engineered another scoring drive. Tim Smith capped off that drive with a 58-yard TD scamper.

Before the day was over, the Redskins had not only destroyed the Broncos, 42–10, they had also set three Super Bowl records that still stand today: most total yards in a game (602); most points in a quarter (35); most yards rushing (Smith, 204). In addition, Doug Williams, who had started the season as a second-string quarterback, proved he was number one.

Key play: Up 10–0, the Broncos kicked off to the Redskins midway through the first period. Washington's Ricky Sanders fumbled the ball, but teammate Ravin Caldwell recovered it. That kept Denver from scoring again quickly and taking over the game.

Statistics of Super Bowl XXII

SCORE BY PERIODS

Denver Broncos (AFC)	10	0	0	0—10
Washington Redskins (NFC)	0	35	0	7—42

SCORING

Denver—Nattiel 56 pass from Elway (Karlis kick)

Denver—Karlis field goal (24)

Washington—Sanders 80 pass from Williams (Haji-Sheikh kick)

Washington—Clark 27 pass from Williams (Haji-Sheikh kick)

Washington—Smith 58 run (Haji-Sheikh kick)

Washington—Sanders 50 pass from Williams (Haji-Sheikh kick)

Washington—Didier 8 pass from Williams (Haji-Sheikh kick)

Washington—Smith 4 run (Haji-Sheikh kick)

KEY TEAM STATISTICS

	Denver	Washington
Yards gained rushing	97	280
Yards gained passing	230	322
Total yards gained	327	602
Interceptions thrown	3	1
Fumbles lost	0	0
Total turnovers	3	1
Number of times sacked	5	2
Yardage lost via sacks	50	18

KEY INDIVIDUAL STATISTICS

Denver

Leading Passer:	Elway	14–38, 257 yards, 1 TD, 3 int.
Leading Rusher:	Lang	5 carries for 38 yards
Leading Receivers:	Jackson	4 for 76 yards
	Nattiel	2 for 69 yards, 1 TD
Kicker:	Karlis	1–1 PAT, 1–2 field goals

Washington

Leading Passer:	Williams	18–29, 340 yards, 4 TD, 1 int.
Leading Rusher:	Smith	22 carries for 204 yards, 2 TD
Leading Receiver:	Sanders	9 for 193, 2 TD
Defensive Leader:	Wilburn	2 int. (11 yards)
Kicker:	Haji-Sheikh	6–6 PAT, 0–1 field goals

70

Super Bowl XXIII—
Joe Montana, Superman

January 22, 1989—Miami, Florida

If you were going to invent the perfect championship football game, what would you include? You would want to have two great quarterbacks going against each other. You would want outstanding plays on both offense and defense by each team. You would probably have the game start off slowly and then become more and more exciting, with the score always staying close. You would want the momentum to go from one team to the other. You would have a hero come in and direct a heart-stopping final drive for the victory. Put all of that together, and you have Super Bowl XXIII.

The San Francisco 49ers and Cincinnati Bengals were facing each other for the second time in a Super Bowl. They had played an exciting, close game seven years before.

The two clubs were alike in many ways. Their quarterbacks, Joe Montana and Boomer Esiason, loved to use short passes to control the offense. They had great receivers—Jerry Rice for the 49ers and Eddie Brown for the Bengals. Each had an outstanding runner—Roger Craig for the 49ers and Ickey Woods for the Bengals. And both their defenses were tough. It looked like a good matchup.

The game was a defensive battle for the first half. The 49ers scored first on an opening-quarter field goal by Mike Cofer. The Bengals tied it up on a Jim Breech field goal in the second period. San Francisco had two other good chances to score, but the Cincinnati defense held each time, and the 49ers came away with no more points.

The Bengals finally got things moving in the third quarter. Esiason clicked on several passes in a row to get his club into 49ers territory. Then he tried a few rushing plays, but the Cincy runners couldn't penetrate San Francisco's defense. The Bengals settled for another field goal and a 6–3 lead. The Bengals got the ball right back, but a pass interception helped set up San Francisco's tying field goal a few minutes later.

The game was almost three-fourths over, and there had still been no touchdowns. Then Cincinnati's outstanding kick returner Stanford Jennings took Mike Cofer's kickoff on the 7-yard line and raced through the middle of the San Francisco defenders. No one touched him, and he didn't even have to change direction. He just moved in a straight line for a 93-yard touchdown—the second longest in Super Bowl history.

Cincinnati fans almost didn't have time to celebrate, however. It took Joe Montana only four plays to move his club 85 yards and even the score. He passed 31 yards to Rice, 40 to Craig, and 14 to Rice again for the tying TD. But the Bengals were able to come back again. Esiason directed a slow, 11-play drive to the 49ers' 22-yard line. From there, Breech kicked a field goal to put Cincy ahead 16–13 with three minutes to go in the game. "Right then, I felt we were going to win it," said the Bengals' All-Star tackle Anthony Munoz. He was wrong.

Montana wasn't nervous as he gathered his teammates around him and called two plays at a time to save precious seconds. He threw four straight complete passes and then tried a running play for another first down. Two more completions . . . an incompletion to stop the clock . . . another completion that was called back because of a penalty . . . a long pass to Rice . . . a short pass to Craig. That put the ball on the 10-yard line with 39 seconds to go.

On the next play, two San Francisco receivers set up wrong. They should have been on opposite sides of the line, not the same side, and it looked like a potential disaster. But nothing could stop Joe Montana. He took the snap, looked from side to side for an open receiver, and then whipped a strike to John Taylor in the end zone. Touchdown! Joe Montana had done it again.

As the 49ers began their final drive, one Cincy player told a teammate, "We've got them now." The teammate replied, "Not really. Have you taken a look at who's quarterbacking that team? Joe Montana is not human." The Bengal teammate was right: in the Super Bowl, Joe Montana is "Superman."

Key play: During the 49ers' quick scoring drive early in the fourth period, Montana completed three passes in four plays. The one incompletion should have been an interception. Bengal defender Lewis Billups dropped the ball in the end zone. On the next play, Montana hit Rice for the touchdown.

Statistics of Super Bowl XXIII

SCORE BY PERIODS

Cincinnati Bengals (AFC)	0	3	10	3—16
San Francisco 49ers (NFC)	3	0	3	14—20

SCORING

San Francisco—Cofer field goal (41)
Cincinnati—Breech field goal (34)
Cincinnati—Breech field goal (43)
San Francisco—Cofer field goal (32)
Cincinnati—Jennings 93 kickoff return (Breech kick)
San Francisco—Rice 14 pass from Montana (Cofer kick)
Cincinnati—Breech field goal (40)
San Francisco—Taylor 10 pass from Montana (Cofer kick)

KEY TEAM STATISTICS

	Cincinnati	San Francisco
Yards gained rushing	106	111
Yards gained passing	123	343
Total yards gained	229	454
Interceptions thrown	1	0
Fumbles lost	0	1
Total turnovers	1	1
Number of times sacked	5	3
Yardage lost via sacks	21	14

KEY INDIVIDUAL STATISTICS
Cincinnati

Leading Passer:	Esiason	11–25, 144 yards, 0 TD, 1 int.
Leading Rusher:	Woods	20 carries for 79 yards
Leading Receiver:	Brown	4 for 44 yards
Kicker:	Breech	1–1 PAT, 3–3 field goals

San Francisco

Leading Passer:	Montana	23–36, 357 yards, 2 TD, 0 int.
Leading Rusher:	Craig	17 carries for 74 yards
Leading Receivers:	Rice	11 for 215 yards, 1 TD
	Craig	8 for 101 yards
Defensive Leader:	Haley	2 sacks for 10 yards
Kicker:	Cofer	2–2 PAT, 2–4 field goals

Super Bowl XXIV—Number 4 for the 49ers
January 28, 1990—New Orleans, Louisiana

Coming into Super Bowl XXIV, the San Francisco 49ers had played in three Super Bowls and had won all three. The Denver Broncos had played in three Super Bowls and had lost all three. So it was not surprising that the 49ers were a big favorite to beat the Broncos this year.

Joe Montana and Jerry Rice, two San Francisco heroes of Super Bowl XXIII a year earlier, were ready to go again. Midway through the first quarter, they combined on a 20-yard touchdown pass that put the 49ers ahead 7–0. It was the first of three Montana-to-Rice scoring strikes for the day.

The Broncos came back a few minutes later on a long David Treadwell field goal that made the score 7–3. Denver fans clapped loudly, but they wouldn't have much else to cheer about. The San Francisco defenders simply shut down Denver quarterback John Elway, one of the best passers in football. Whenever Elway stepped back to pass, he was surrounded by big defensive linemen. He was sacked six times and forced to throw passes before he was ready lots of other times.

Meanwhile, the 49ers' offense was unstoppable. They led the Broncos 27–3 by halftime and 41–10 after three quarters. Montana and his teammates set several scoring records during the game. They totaled 55 points and eight touchdowns, the most ever in a Super Bowl. They also beat Denver by 45 points, 55–10, the largest margin of victory of all time. Montana threw five touchdown passes, and kicker Mike Cofer was successful on seven points after touchdowns, both records.

Denver's defensive coach Wade Phillips said, "The most we gave up all year was 28 points. Today, the 49ers got 27 in the first half and 28 more in the second half. They have a great killer instinct. You make a mistake, and they go for the big play."

With the victory, San Francisco joined Pittsburgh as the only teams in football history to win four Super Bowls. With the loss, Denver tied Minnesota as the only teams to lose four Super Bowls.

Key play: During the first quarter, Denver was behind by only 7–3. The Broncos were moving toward a score. Halfback Bobby Humphrey was hit hard as he ran with the ball and fumbled. The 49ers then drove down for a touchdown, and Denver never could catch up again.

Statistics of Super Bowl XXIV

SCORE BY PERIODS

Denver Broncos (AFC)	3	0	7	0—10
San Francisco 49ers (NFC)	13	14	14	14—55

SCORING
San Francisco—Rice 20 pass from Montana (Cofer kick)
Denver—Treadway field goal (42)
San Francisco—Jones 7 pass from Montana (kick failed)
San Francisco—Cofer field goal (32)
San Francisco—Rathman 1 run (Cofer kick)
San Francisco—Rice 38 pass from Montana (Cofer kick)
San Francisco—Rice 28 pass from Montana (Cofer kick)
San Francisco—Taylor 35 pass from Montana (Cofer kick)
Denver—Elway 3 run (Treadway kick)
San Francisco—Rathman 3 run (Cofer kick)
San Francisco—Craig 1 run (Cofer kick)

KEY TEAM STATISTICS

	Denver	San Francisco
Yards gained rushing	64	144
Yards gained passing	103	317
Total yards gained	167	461
Interceptions thrown	2	0
Fumbles lost	2	0
Total turnovers	4	0
Number of times sacked	6	1
Yardage lost via sacks	33	0

KEY INDIVIDUAL STATISTICS
Denver

Leading Passer:	Elway	10–26, 108 yards, 0 TD, 2 int.
Leading Rusher:	Humphrey	12 carries for 61 yards
Leading Receiver:	Humphrey	3 for 38 yards
Kicker:	Treadwell	1–1 PAT, 1–1 field goals

San Francisco

Leading Passer:	Montana	22–29, 297 yards, 5 TD, 0 int.
Leading Rushers:	Craig	30 carries for 69 yards, 1 TD
	Rathman	11 carries for 38 yards, 2 TD
Leading Receivers:	Rice	7 for 148 yards, 3 TD
	Craig	5 for 34 yards
Defensive Leader:	Stubbs	2 sacks for 7 yards
Kicker:	Cofer	7–8 PAT, 0–0 field goals

Super Bowl XXV—One Giant Point
January 27, 1991—Tampa, Florida

The Buffalo Bills had been one of the top teams in the old American Football League. They had won two AFL championships before the AFL and NFL merged. But the Bills had not been as successful after that and had never made it to a Super Bowl. By the 1990 season, Buffalo had become one of the best-balanced teams in football. Their offense, led by quarterback Jim Kelly and halfback Thurman Thomas, scored quickly and often. Their defense, featuring All-Stars Bruce Smith and Cornelius Bennett, was tough and powerful. The Bills ended with a 13–3 record, tops in the AFC. One win was a 17–13 thriller over the New York Giants late in the year. Now Buffalo was ready to play the Giants again in Super Bowl XXV.

The Giants had a mixed-up year. They began the season with a 10–0 record. Then starting quarterback Phil Simms got hurt. His replacement, Jeff Hostetler, took a while to get used to his new role as a starter, and New York lost three of its last four games. In the playoffs, however, Hostetler was outstanding, and the Giants edged San Francisco in the NFC title game to earn a place in the Super Bowl.

New York had two main weapons. Its defense was one of the best in football. Leading the way was Lawrence Taylor, perhaps the finest linebacker of all time. On offense the Giants liked to control the ball with running plays that used up a lot of time. That was their plan in Super Bowl XXV. They figured that by running a lot, they could keep Buffalo's high-scoring offense off the field and win the game.

New York opened the contest with a typical slow drive that ended with a Matt Bahr field goal to put the Giants ahead 3–0. Buffalo struck back quickly. Kelly threw a 61-yard pass to James Lofton to move the Bills near the Giants' goal line. But Buffalo couldn't penetrate the New York defense for a touchdown and had to settle for a tying field goal by kicker Scott Norwood.

The game seesawed back and forth, with Buffalo ahead 12–10 at halftime. In the third period, New York got the ball again and kept it for a long time. The Giants took almost ten minutes to score a go-ahead touchdown and gain a 17–12 lead. Once again, Buffalo came back quickly. The Bills scored on the first play of the fourth quarter to go back on top, 19–17.

You can probably guess what happened next. The Giants made another long drive. With less than four minutes to go in the game, Bahr kicked another field goal, and New York had a 20–19 lead.

Now it was Kelly's turn again. He led the Bills from their own 10-yard line to the Giants' 29. With only eight seconds left, Scott Norwood came in to attempt a winning 47-yard field goal. His kick started out perfectly, then slid a little too far to the right. Giants fans breathed a sigh of relief; Buffalo fans were brokenhearted. The 20–19 final score was the closest ever in a Super Bowl.

Key play: During the Giants' third-period drive, Buffalo's defense had them stopped. Then Hostetler completed a long pass to Mark Ingram on third down to keep the drive alive and help New York regain the lead.

Statistics of Super Bowl XXV

SCORE BY PERIODS

Buffalo Bills (AFC)	3	9	0	7—19
New York Giants (NFC)	3	7	7	3—20

SCORING
New York—Bahr field goal (28)
Buffalo—Norwood field goal (23)
Buffalo—D. Smith 1 run (Norwood kick)
Buffalo—safety, Hostetler tackled by B. Smith in end zone
New York—Baker 14 pass from Hostetler (Bahr kick)
New York—Anderson 1 run (Bahr kick)
Buffalo—Thomas 31 run (Norwood kick)
New York—Bahr field goal (21)

KEY TEAM STATISTICS

	Buffalo	New York
Yards gained rushing	166	172
Yards gained passing	205	214
Total yards gained	371	386
Interceptions thrown	0	0
Fumbles lost	0	0
Total turnovers	0	0

| Number of times sacked | 1 | 2 |
| Yardage lost via sacks | 7 | 8 |

KEY INDIVIDUAL STATISTICS
Buffalo
Leading Passer:	Kelly	18–30, 212 yards, 0 TD, 0 int.
Leading Rusher:	Thomas	15 carries for 135 yards, 1 TD
Leading Receiver:	Reed	8 for 62 yards
Defensive Leader:	B. Smith	sacked Hostetler for safety
Kicker:	Norwood	2–2 PAT, 1–2 field goals

New York
Leading Passer:	Hostetler	20–32, 222 yards, 1 TD, 0 int.
Leading Rusher:	Anderson	21 carries for 102 yards, 1 TD
Leading Receivers:	Ingram	5 for 74 yards
	Bavaro	5 for 50 yards
Defensive Leader:	Marshall	1 sack for 7 yards
Kicker:	Cofer	2–2 PAT, 2–2 field goals

Super Bowl XXVI—Rypien Rips the Bills
January 26, 1992—Minneapolis, Minnesota

Buffalo was back in Super Bowl XXVI for a second straight try to win the NFL championship. This time, their opponents were the Washington Redskins, whose record in Super Bowls stood at 2–2.

Buffalo quarterback Jim Kelly summed up his team's feelings about the upcoming game. "I've been dreaming about playing in the Super Bowl since I was a kid, and I got the chance last year. But now I want to be a winner. That's the only thing that counts."

Like Kelly, all of the Bills were feeling a lot of pressure as they prepared for the Super Bowl, and it showed. They yelled a lot at each other and at their coaches.

Meanwhile, the Redskins were all business. They were an outstanding all-around team. Their offense, led by young quarterback Mark Rypien, had scored more points than any other NFL club, and their defense was ranked third in the league. The 'Skins had compiled a 14–2 record during the regular season and had destroyed the Detroit Lions in the NFC title game, 41–10.

Washington used its balance to control the game in the first half. On offense, Rypien completed several big passes and handed off for slashing runs by Ricky Ervins and Gerald Riggs to help the Redskins score 17 points in the second quarter. On defense, Washington tried some special plays to stop running back Thurman Thomas, the league's Most Valuable Player in 1991. Thomas gained only 13 yards on ten carries in the entire game. The Redskins also put a big rush on Jim Kelly and forced him to make lots of mistakes. Kelly became more and more frustrated as the game went on.

Washington added a touchdown early in the second half, following an interception of a pass that Kelly had rushed too much. The score was 24–0, and Buffalo players and their fans were shocked. The Bills finally managed to get their offense going and scored 10 points quickly to cut the lead to 24–10. If their defense could just hold the Redskins now, then the Bills might just win this game.

But the defense couldn't hold. Rypien led Washington on a terrific 11-play drive. He threw some bullet passes, and Ervins ran over Buffalo tacklers for big gains. Before the end of the quarter, Washington scored again to take a commanding lead. When the final gun sounded, the score was 37–24, with the Redskins on top.

81

Key play: During Washington's big drive at the end of the third period, wide receiver Gary Clark faked his defender out of position and broke open for a 30-yard touchdown. That score sank the Bills' hopes for a comeback.

Statistics of Super Bowl XXVI

SCORE BY PERIODS

Buffalo Bills (AFC)	0	0	10	14—24
Washington Redskins (NFC)	0	17	14	6—37

SCORING

Washington—Lohmiller field goal (34)
Washington—Byner 10 pass from Rypien (Lohmiller kick)
Washington—Riggs 1 run (Lohmiller kick)
Washington—Riggs 2 run (Lohmiller kick)
Buffalo—Norwood field goal (21)
Buffalo—Thomas 1 run (Norwood kick)
Washington—Clark 30 pass from Rypien (Lohmiller kick)
Washington—Lohmiller field goal (25)
Washington—Lohmiller field goal (39)
Buffalo—Metzelaars 2 pass from Kelly (Norwood kick)
Buffalo—Beebe 4 pass from Kelly (Norwood kick)

KEY TEAM STATISTICS

	Buffalo	Washington
Yards gained rushing	43	125
Yards gained passing	240	292
Total yards gained	283	417
Interceptions thrown	4	1
Fumbles lost	1	0
Total turnovers	5	1
Number of times sacked	5	0
Yardage lost via sacks	46	0

KEY INDIVIDUAL STATISTICS
Buffalo
Leading Passer:	Kelly	28–58, 275 yards, 2 TD, 4 int.
Leading Rusher:	Thomas	10 carries for 13 yards, 1 TD
Leading Receiver:	Lofton	7 for 92 yards
Kicker:	Norwood	3–3 PAT, 1–1 field goal

Washington
Leading Passer:	Rypien	18–33, 292 yards, 2 TD, 1 int.
Leading Rushers:	Ervins	13 carries for 72 yards
	Riggs	5 carries for 7 yards, 2 TD
Leading Receivers:	Clark	7 for 114 yards, 1 TD
	Monk	7 for 113 yards
Defensive Leader:	Edwards	2 int. (56 yards)
Kicker:	Lohmiller	4–4 PAT, 3–3 field goals

Super Bowl XXVII—
The Cowboys Rope Buffalo

January 31, 1993—Pasadena, California

The biggest news about Super Bowl XXVII was that the Dallas Cowboys were back. Dallas had not played on Super Sunday since 1979. In the 14 years since, the team had fallen on hard times. Finally in 1989 a new owner named Jerry Jones took over. Jones hired his close friend Jimmie Johnson, a top college coach, to run the team and fired almost everyone else, including many players.

The "newly remodeled" Cowboys had the worst record in the league in 1989, 1–15. Four years later, however, they were conference champs. The team leaders were an outstanding young quarterback named Troy Aikman and the best running back in football, Emmitt Smith.

There was another club making a return in Super Bowl XXVII—the Buffalo Bills. They were appearing in a third straight Super Bowl but were still looking for their first NFL championship. Buffalo's veteran leaders—Jim Kelly, Thurman Thomas, and Bruce Smith—were feeling lots of pressure to win and finally end their Super Bowl jinx.

Sports reporters had mixed opinions about who would capture the upcoming game. They noted that Dallas was younger and quicker than Buffalo and had a better mix of offensive power and defensive strength. The Bills, on the other hand, had more experience and would probably not be as nervous playing in the big game.

The Cowboys did seem a little nervous at the beginning. The Bills' defense held Dallas and forced a punt that Buffalo's Steve Tasker blocked. Four plays later, Thomas raced into the end zone with the first score of the day.

Dallas struck back quickly at the end of the first period. Aikman completed a touchdown pass to tight end Jay Novacek. Then the Cowboys kicked off. On Buffalo's next offensive play, Kelly was hit hard and fumbled. Dallas's Jimmy Jones caught the ball in the air and raced into the end zone. Dallas had scored 14 points in 15 seconds!

A few minutes later, Buffalo had one more chance to take control of the game. A long pass from Kelly to receiver Andre Reed put the ball on the Dallas 4-yard line. Two running plays got Buffalo near the goal line, but the Cowboys would not let the Bills score. Defensive back Thomas Everett intercepted a Kelly pass in the end zone, and snuffed out the Buffalo threat.

From then on, the game belonged to the Cowboys. They ran up 14 points in the second quarter and 21 more in the last period on their way to a 52–17 rout of the Bills. Even a new Buffalo quarterback, Frank Reich, was unable to turn the tide. For Dallas, it was Super Bowl win number three in their history. For Buffalo, it was their third straight Super Bowl loss.

Key play: When Jim Kelly threw the interception in the second quarter, he was expecting Dallas to line up in a different type of defense. The new defense forced Kelly to throw a difficult pass to his receiver and led to the turnover.

Statistics of Super Bowl XXVII

SCORE BY PERIODS

Buffalo Bills (AFC)	7	3	7	0—17
Dallas Cowboys (NFC)	14	14	3	21—52

SCORING
Buffalo—Thomas 2 run (Christie kick)
Dallas—Novacek 23 pass from Aikman (Elliot kick)
Dallas—J. Jones 2 fumble return (Elliot kick)
Buffalo—Christie field goal (21)
Dallas—Irvin 19 pass from Aikman (Elliot kick)
Dallas—Irvin 18 pass from Aikman (Elliot kick)
Dallas—Elliot field goal (20)
Buffalo—Beebe 40 pass from Reich (Christie kick)
Dallas—Harper 45 pass from Aikman (Elliot kick)
Dallas—E. Smith 10 run (Elliot kick)
Dallas—Norton 9 fumble return (Elliot kick)

KEY TEAM STATISTICS

	Buffalo	Dallas
Yards gained rushing	108	137
Yards gained passing	254	271
Total yards gained	362	408
Interceptions thrown	4	0
Fumbles lost	5	2
Total turnovers	9	2

| Number of times sacked | 4 | 1 |
| Yardage lost via sacks | 22 | 2 |

KEY INDIVIDUAL STATISTICS
Buffalo

Leading Passer:	Reich	18–31, 194 yards, 1 TD, 2 int.
Leading Rusher:	Davis	15 carries for 86 yards
Leading Receiver:	Reed	8 for 152 yards
Kicker:	Christie	2–2 PAT, 1–1 field goals

Dallas

Leading Passer:	Aikman	22–30, 273 yards, 4 TD, 0 int.
Leading Rusher:	E. Smith	22 carries for 108 yards, 1 TD
Leading Receivers:	Irvin	6 for 114 yards, 2 TD
	Novacek	7 for 72 yards
Defensive Leader:	J. Jones	2 fumble recoveries, 1 TD
Kicker:	Elliot	7–7 PAT, 1–1 field goals

Super Bowl XXVIII— Cowboys Rope Buffalo, Part 2

January 30, 1994—Atlanta, Georgia

Super Bowl XXVIII was played in a brand new location, the Georgia Dome in Atlanta. But some things about the game seemed very similar to Super Bowl XXVII. Once again, the Dallas Cowboys were competing against the Buffalo Bills. And, for the second year in a row, the Cowboys were favored to capture the NFL championship.

Some football fans kidded Buffalo players because they had lost in three straight Super Bowls. The Bills correctly pointed out that playing on Super Sunday one time was special, but four times was extraordinary. The players felt they should be praised instead of put down. They were determined to prove themselves on the field.

The game got off to an exciting beginning. Dallas's Kevin Williams returned the opening kickoff 50 yards to put the Cowboys in good field position. The Bills' defense held, however, and Eddie Murray kicked a 41-yard field goal to put Dallas ahead, 3–0. Buffalo came right back with a drive of its own that ended with a record 54-yard field goal by Steve Christie to tie the score. During the rest of the first half, Buffalo outscored Dallas 10–3 to take a 7-point lead at intermission.

The second half was an entirely different story. Dallas halfback Emmitt Smith, the league's Most Valuable Player during the season, went up to his offensive coach at halftime. He said, "Get me the ball." That's just what the Cowboys did. On one Dallas drive early in the third period, Smith carried the ball on seven out of eight plays, including a 15-yard touchdown run. On a later drive, he carried on eight of ten plays and another touchdown. Smith was named the game's Most Valuable Player, but he gave much of the credit to the Cowboys' huge offensive linemen, whose blocking opened up big holes for him in the Buffalo defense.

The Dallas defensive unit also deserved a lot of praise. They bottled up Buffalo quarterback Jim Kelly and his receivers all day. They also held Thurman Thomas, the Bill's All-Star halfback, to only 37 yards rushing on 16 carries. The Bills did not score at all in the second half and lost the game, 30–13.

Buffalo had now lost four straight Super Bowls. No other team had ever done that. But the Bills weren't ready to give up. "It's frustrating," said Kelly, "but I still have a couple of years left, so don't count me out. We'll just have to keep coming back until we get this thing right."

Key play: At the start of the second half, Thurman Thomas was tackled hard and fumbled. Dallas's James Washington picked up the ball and raced 46 yards for a touchdown to tie the score at 13–13. That play sparked the Cowboys' turnaround.

Statistics of Super Bowl XXVIII

SCORE BY PERIODS

Buffalo Bills (AFC)	3	10	0	0—13
Dallas Cowboys (NFC)	6	0	14	10—30

SCORING

Dallas—Murray field goal (41)
Buffalo—Christie field goal (54)
Dallas—Murray field goal (24)
Buffalo—T. Thomas 4 run (Christie kick)
Buffalo—Christie field goal (28)
Dallas—J. Washington 46 fumble return (Murray kick)
Dallas—E. Smith 15 run (Murray kick)
Dallas—E. Smith 1 run (Murray kick)
Dallas—Murray field goal (20)

KEY TEAM STATISTICS

	Buffalo	Dallas
Yards gained rushing	87	137
Yards gained passing	227	204
Total yards gained	314	341
Interceptions thrown	1	1
Fumbles lost	2	0
Total turnovers	3	1
Number of times sacked	3	2
Yardage lost via sacks	33	3

KEY INDIVIDUAL STATISTICS
Buffalo
Leading Passer:	Kelly	31–50, 260 yards, 0 TD, 1 int.
Leading Rusher:	T. Thomas	16 carries for 37 yards, 1 TD
Leading Receivers:	Brooks	7 for 63 yards
	T. Thomas	7 for 52 yards
Defensive Leader:	Odomes	1 int. (41 yards)
Kicker:	Christie	1–1 PAT, 2–2 field goals

Dallas
Leading Passer:	Aikman	19–27, 207 yards, 0 TD, 1 int.
Leading Rusher:	E. Smith	30 carries for 132 yards, 2 TD
Leading Receivers:	Irvin	5 for 66 yards
	Novacek	5 for 26 yards
Defensive Leader:	Washington	1 fumble recovery (TD), 1 int.
Kicker:	Murray	3–3 PAT, 3–3 field goals

Super Bowl Record Book

Individual Records
Passing Records
(Super Bowl number is listed in parentheses.)

Most passes attempted in a career	Jim Kelly	145
Most passes attempted in a game	Jim Kelly (XXVI)	58
Most passes completed in a career	Joe Montana	83
Most passes completed in a game	Jim Kelly (XXVIII)	31
Most yards gained passing in a game	Joe Montana (XXIII)	357
Best completion percentage in a game	Phil Simms (XXI)	88%
Most touchdown passes in a career	Joe Montana	11
Most touchdown passes in a game	Joe Montana (XXIV)	5
Most interceptions thrown in a game	Craig Morton (XII)	4
	Jim Kelly (XXVI)	4

Rushing Records
(Super Bowl number is listed in parentheses.)

Most rushing attempts in a career	Franco Harris	101
Most rushing attempts in a game	John Riggins (XVII)	38
Most yards gained rushing in a career	Franco Harris	354
Most yards gained rushing in a game	Timmy Smith (XXII)	204
Most yards gained on one run	Marcus Allen (XVIII)	74
Most rushing touchdowns in a career	Franco Harris	4
	Thurman Thomas	4
Most rushing touchdowns in a game	ten players	2

Pass Receiving Records
(Super Bowl number is listed in parentheses.)

Most receptions in a career	Andre Reed	27
Most receptions in a game	Dan Ross (XVI)	11
	Jerry Rice (XXIII)	11
Most yards gained in a career	Lynn Swann	364
Most yards gained in a game	Jerry Rice (XXIII)	215
Most yards gained on a reception	Kenny King (XV)	80
	Ricky Sanders (XXII)	80
Most touchdowns in a career	Jerry Rice	4
Most touchdowns in a game	Jerry Rice (XXIV)	3

Kicking Records

(Super Bowl number is listed in parentheses.)

Most points scored kicking in a career	Ray Wersching	22
Most points scored kicking in a game	Don Chandler (II)	15
Most accurate field-goal kicker (career)	Ray Wersching	5–5
Longest field goal	Steve Christie (XXVIII)	54
Shortest field goal missed	Mike Cofer (XXIII)	19

Team Records

(Super Bowl number is listed in parentheses.)

Most games played	Dallas	7
Most games played in a row	Buffalo	4
Most games won	Pittsburgh	4
	San Francisco	4
	Dallas	4
Most games lost	Minnesota	4
	Denver	4
	Buffalo	4
Most points scored in a game	San Francisco (XXIV)	55
Fewest points scored in a game	Miami (VI)	3
Most touchdowns in a game	San Francisco (XXIV)	8
Most yards gained passing in a game	San Francisco (XXIII)	343
Most yards gained rushing in a game	Washington (XXII)	280
Most total yards gained in a game	Washington (XXII)	602

Most passing touchdowns in a game	San Francisco (XXIV)	5
Most rushing touchdowns in a game	Chicago (XX)	4
Fewest total yards gained in a game	Minnesota (IX)	119
Fewest yards gained rushing in a game	New England (XX)	7
Fewest yards gained passing in a game	Denver (XII)	35
Most turnovers in a game	Buffalo (XXVII)	9

Coaching records

Don Shula has coached the most Super Bowl teams (six—one with Baltimore and five with Miami).

Chuck Noll has been the winning coach the most times (four—all with Pittsburgh).

Bud Grant (Minnesota) and Marv Levy (Buffalo) have been the losing coaches the most times—four.